THE ORIGIN

OF THE

Disciples of Christ

By
William H. Whitsitt, DD, LLD

With a Review and Rebuttal of Whisitt's Falsehoods by
George W. Longan

Charleston, AR:
COBB PUBLISHING
2024

Publisher's Preface

What you now hold in your hands (or read on your screen) is a unique volume. In 1888, William H. Whitsitt, a professor in the Southern Baptist Theological Seminary published a book, *Origin of the Disciples of Christ,* which he subtitled "A Contribution to the Centennial Anniversary of the Birth of Alexander Campbell."

The next year, George W. Longan published a book of the same title, as a rebuttal to Whitsitt's book. Of special interest is the appendix he included, which includes reviews of Whitsitt's book by some of his contemporary Baptist brethren.

We include both books in this one volume for the sake of convenience for those interested.

No changes were made to the text of the original books. All of the original footnotes to these books are included. Items *within the text* which are contained in brackets [ ] appeared that way original book

Some footnotes have been added to this edition to (1) give definitions of older words, or (2) to give Bible references which deal with the subject being discussed. These new footnotes are contained within brackets [ ].

Bradley S. Cobb
2020

Contents

ORIGIN

OF THE
DISCIPLES OF CHRIST

(CAMPBELLITES)

A CONTRIBUTION TO THE CENTENNIAL ANNIVERSARY OF
THE BIRTH OF ALEXANDER CAMPBELL

BY

WILLIAM H. WHITSITT, D.D., LL.D.

PROFESSOR IN THE
SOUTHERN BAPTIST THEOLOGICAL SEMINARY

1888

CHAPTER I:
THE SANDEMANIANS

The Disciples of Christ — commonly called *Campbellites*, from the name of their founder, Mr. Alexander Campbell of Bethany, West Virginia — are an offshoot of the Sandemanian sect of Scotland. This latter sect was established in the early portion of the eighteenth century by Mr. John Glas, a minister of the Established Church of Scotland. Mr. Glas was placed over the parish of Tealing, near Dundee, Forfarshire, in the year 1719.[1] The region of country in which his residence was situated seems to have been considerably infested by Dissenters of the type called Cameronians, who made a loud noise against the Kirk of Scotland[2] because she had now departed, in some respects, from the letter of the National Covenants, asserting that by this means she had lost the right to be styled a *Church of Christ.*

In order to meet the objections of these adversaries, Mr. Glas resolved to investigate the whole question of national covenanting in the light of the Scriptures. The issue of these researches was different from anything he had anticipated. By means of them he not only withdrew the foundation of strict biblical precept from beneath the feet of the Cameronians, but the supports upon which his own Church was established were, in his judgment, likewise destroyed. These covenants, whether in their ancient or their modern observance, proceeded all alike upon the supposition that a connection between Church and State is in accordance with the teachings of the Sacred Word.[3] On his attaining to the conviction that a union of this nature was not provided for in the New Testament, Mr. Glas became displeased with his own position in the Established Church, as well as with the representations of the Cameronians. He was more than ever confirmed in the resolution "to take to himself no other rule but the word of God."

His reflections upon that Word now speedily made him aware that the rite of communion, as it was observed in his own and other parishes, was not strictly in accordance with the pattern of the apostolical churches. Many persons of the weakest pretensions to pious living, and

---

[1] *Narrative of the Rise and Progress of the Controversy about the National Covenants.* By Mr. John Glas, late Minister of the Gospel at Tealing. Second edition, Dundee, 1828, p. 159.

[2] [The national church of Scotland.]

[3] Glas's *Narrative*, pp. 1-25, also p. 139.

many more who made no claims to any special renewal by the Spirit of holiness, were entitled, in virtue of their birthright, to the benefits of a position at the table of the Lord. This posture of circumstances had become unendurable to him.

Accordingly, on the 13th of July 1725, he sought to relieve his conscience by organizing a conventicle within the boundaries of his parish, composed of those only who he believed had experienced a complete change of heart.[1]

When the literalistic tendency of Mr. Glas had resulted in this *ecclesiola in ecclesia*,[2] it became the means of directing public attention to his proceedings. A communion occasion at Strathmartine, on the 6th of August, 1726, served to bring him face to face with the opposition that was gathering head against him. Echoes of the rising strife were also heard in the Presbytery of Dundee, at its session on the 7th of September following. The affair likewise came to discussion, after an informal fashion, in the Synod of Angus and Mearns when it convened in October 1726.

Nothing of consequence was done in the premises until the 17th of October 1727, at which date the Synod of Angus and Mearns laid upon the Presbytery of Dundee, to which the parish of Tealing belonged, the duty of bringing Mr. Glas to trial at a special session which they should convene for that purpose; and ordered that these in turn should bring the results of their investigations before the Synod at its next session at Brechin in April 1728. This mandate was observed; and after due deliberation was had, the Synod of Angus and Mearns, on the 18th of April 1728, pronounced a sentence of suspension from the ministry against Mr. Glas, for promulgating sentiments hostile to the National Covenants and to the union of Church and State in any form. An appeal was taken to the General Assembly, which convened about a fortnight later, on the 2nd of May, which, however, confirmed the action of the Synod. Meanwhile, Mr. Glas having laid himself liable to the charge of contumacy[3] by continuing to preach the obnoxious doctrine after his suspension from office, a sentence of deposition was passed against him by the Synod in October 1728. An appeal being taken against this new sentence, it was likewise confirmed by decision of the Commission of the

---

[1] *Memoranda of John Glas and Robert Sandeman*, collected from MS. notes of the late James Scott, member of the church in Dundee; in *Letters and Discourses of Robert Sandeman*, Dundee, 1851, p. 118. Compare also Glas's *Narrative*, pp. 103 and 113.

[2] ["Church within a church."]

[3] [Stubbornness.]

Assembly, at a meeting appointed to consider the case, on the 12th of March 1730.[1]

The brief outlines which have just been given will avail, in some sort, to bring before the reader a view of the special occasion that induced Mr. Glas to rebel against the Kirk of Scotland, and of the main incidents of the process that was thereupon entered against him. His own reflections concerning the teachings of the Scriptures had brought him to embrace the position of the English Independents in relation to the question concerning the proper church order, while the action of the constituted authorities had already destroyed his sympathy for the National Establishment.

Though his followers and himself were in the custom of designating themselves, and the churches they subsequently organized, by the name of "Independents,"[2] or sometimes Congregationalists,[3] yet they made no effort to form relations with the people who in England bear those names. On the contrary, they stood wholly aloof; and, guided by the Scriptures, they resolved to work out from this source, alone and without any assistance, the more minute details of the constitution, life, worship, and discipline of the churches of the New Testament period. The passion they had acquired for contradicting the usages and the doctrines of the "popular clergy" was so keen that they were soon driven into excesses; and before they progressed very far there had arisen so large a variety of convictions and usages, that many of the individual bodies differed from each other in regard to a number of particulars, while each single item, though never so insignificant in appearance, was liable to become an occasion of separation.

---

[1] The above facts are taken from, Glas's *Narrative.*

[2] Glas, *Narrative,* p. 110; also *Memoir of Mr. John Glas,* prefixed to the *Narrative,* p. xvii.

[3] *Memoir of Mr. John Glas,* prefixed to *Narrative,* p. xxvi

CHAPTER II:
"THE ANCIENT ORDER OF THINGS"

The tithing of mint, anise, and cumin, it has been suggested, became the principal concern of Mr. Glas and his followers. The work was begun only a few months after the sentence of deposition from the Kirk of Scotland had been confirmed. Mr. Glas had an uncommon amount of confidence in the capacity of the poorest of the brethren to divine the truth of God from the biblical word, and often boasted that he got hints from them which served to open and explain many things which he had not previously understood. During the summer of 1730, while he was absent in the Highlands for the benefit of his health, these humble people raised a scruple in the church over which he now presided in Dundee, regarding the ruling elders, which, as former Presbyterians, they had adopted from the constitution of the Established Church. The pastor was speedily fetched from his summer retreat for the purpose of adjusting the difficulty. This enterprise was accomplished by abolishing the office of ruling elders, and substituting in their stead a plurality of elders, whose duty it should be both to preach and to teach.[1] The fashion of employing a plurality of elders is likewise found among the Disciples of America.

To an aged member of the church, also presumably one of the poorest of the people, is due the innovation of weekly communion in the Lord's Supper. The conventicle[2] which Mr. Glas had gathered around him was at first in the habit of monthly celebrating the Lord's Supper. The person referred to suggested the inquiry why they should meet every month for that purpose, and not once or twice in the year, as the churches of the Establishment were in the custom of doing. A debate was held regarding the business, by means of which it was concluded that both of these practices were without example in the New Testament; and thereupon the weekly service was enjoined.[3] The Disciples also observe this usage.[4]

In the beginning of the movement it was expected that the elders, of whom there were indispensably two or three in every church, should sustain themselves, by their own exertions, in some trade or profession

---

[1] *Memoranda of John Glas and Robert Sandeman*, as found in the *Letters and Discourses of Robert Sandeman*, pp. 118-119.

[2] [A small gathering for religious worship.]

[3] *Memoranda of John Glas and Robert Sandeman*, in the place above cited, p. 119.

[4] [See Acts 20:7, 1 Corinthians 11:17-20.]

outside of the ministry. This peculiarity has been retained, with considerable tenacity, in some of the Sandemanian churches.[1] The early Disciples, in their turn, laid much stress upon this point;[2] but of late they are becoming less strenuous regarding it.

Seeing that he was now fairly launched upon a career of literalism, Mr. Glas would soon perceive that it was impossible to find in the New Testament writings any documents like the Longer and Shorter Catechisms of the Kirk of Scotland. Accordingly, in the year 1736, he published a pamphlet under the title of *"The Usefulness of Catechisms Considered,"* and takes the occasion to discourage the employment of them by his followers. The Confession of Faith, in its turn, was abolished. Besides the fact that there was directly no Divine command enjoining its existence, the Westminster Confession had been, in some sort, the occasion of his displacement from the parish at Tealing.

The attention of the party was soon directed to the love-feast which prevailed in the early Christian Church; and, with the courage of their convictions, this observance was also added as an indispensable mark of a genuine Church of Christ. Their successors in England are quite as stringent as were the Sandemanians of the eighteenth century in requiring the presence of each and every member on these occasions.[3] Mr. Campbell, the founder of the Disciples, seriously considered this matter; but, while he allowed that the custom was of biblical authority, and might be "found useful when the ancient order of things is restored,"[4] he yet lacked a sufficient amount of courage to enjoin the observance of it. On the other hand, he was fully as clear as the Sandemanians in his denunciations of church catechisms, creeds, and confessions of faith.

The Sandemanians were easily able to discover that the kiss of charity was several times enjoined in the apostolical letters, and hence this observance was frequently found among them. Mr. Campbell's courage and devotion to the distinct commands of the word of God failed him entirely at this point.[5]

The conditions were almost the same in the case of feet-washing.

---

[1] *An Account of the Christian Practices of the Church in Barnsbury Grove,* Barnsbury, London, 1878, p. 10.

[2] *Christian Baptist,* edit. 6, p. 91, pp. 28- 29, 48, 37, 46.

[3] *Barnsbury Grove,* as above, p. 10.

[4] *Christian Baptist,* edit. 6, pp. 283-284

[5] *Christian Baptist,* edit. 6, 224. Compare also Richardson, vol. 2. p. 129, where Mr. Campbell had an opportunity to resist this observance in a small church at Pittsburg, which professed Sandemanian views.

This practice was also regarded by numbers of the Sandemanians as an important mark of a true Church of Christ. It is still observed by them,[1] but they do not now appear to consider it of the same binding necessity as formerly. Mr. Campbell rejected it entirely as a church observance,[2] though he was not averse that it should be performed as an expression of private hospitality.

The Sandemanians early became convinced that it was an article of capital concern, that their adherents should abstain from eating blood. In this connection they insisted upon the letter of the passage at Acts 15:20, 28-29. No distinct allusion, on the part of the Disciples, to the binding force of this apostolical prohibition, can be remembered.

The Sandemanians laid unusual stress upon the intercessory prayer of our Lord, in the seventeenth chapter of the Gospel according to John; holding that it inculcates[3] the necessity of absolute unanimity, on the part of the various members, in every transaction by an individual church. In order to obtain this indispensable unanimity, the parties who may entertain such objections as they are unable to surrender are incontinently[4] expelled from the communion.[5] The Disciples likewise insist with earnestness upon the passage in question; but they understand that it refers to the organic union of all who profess and call themselves Christians, on the basis of the plea which themselves have a charge to urge upon the attention of the religious public.

A modified type of communism prevailed, and is still professed, among the Sandemanians.[6] The personal estate of a communicant could be retained by him after entering the fraternity, but always with the understanding that it was subject to the demands of the necessitous,[7] especially those of them who chanced to be of the household of faith. Accordingly it was expected that their brethren should not lay up any further treasures on earth than such as they were possessed of at the time of their reception.[8] In order to prevent this from taking place, the surplus above their actual necessities in the way of subsistence was to be contributed to the "Fellowship," which is the name they derived from Acts

---

[1] *Barnsbury Grove*, p. 8.
[2] *Christian Baptist*, pp. 222-223
[3] [Teaches.]
[4] [Immediately.]
[5] *Barnsbury Grove*, p. 14.
[6] Richardson, vol. 1. p. 71.
[7] [Those in need.]
[8] Andrew Fuller, *Strictures on Sandemanianism*, Letter IX.

2:42, for the collection for the poor.[1] The Disciples, on the contrary, have never pressed the principle of communism to the same extent; but they have adopted the nomenclature of the Sandemanians in the matter of the weekly collection,[2] which is ordinarily designated as "the Fellowship " in their literature.[3]

The custom of mutual exhortation, as a regular part of religious worship, was in vogue among many of the Sandemanian fraternities. They justified this proceeding by a literal interpretation of 1 Cor. 14:31. It was often assigned a place in the observances of the Sabbath day; but the church of Barnsbury Grove, London, has now removed it to the Wednesday evening meeting.[4]

The business of exhortation was likewise attended to in the first church that was organized by the Disciples in America, as also in the kindred Sandemanian church under the charge of Walter Scott in Pittsburgh, Penn.; but so many evils grew out of it, that after a series of years Mr. Campbell became impatient of it, and succeeded in persuading his followers to surrender their liberty in this regard.[5]

A portion of the Sandemanian fraternity were so strict in their literalism, that, because there is no direct injunction commanding the observance of family prayer, and because there is a Divine command to enter into the closet and pray in secret, they would inveigh against this practice as savoring of a tendency to proselytism.[6] Others of the party discouraged the habit of family prayer, on the ground that it is "unlawful, provided any part of the family be unbelievers, seeing it is holding communion with them."[7]

In his earlier years Mr. Campbell was influenced by this latter view of the subject, and at one time seriously proposed to his father the inquiry "whether family prayer is proper in a family composed in part of unbelievers."[8] Unlike the Sandemanians, however, who could find "no pre-

---

[1] *Barnsbury Grove*, pp. 6-7, also pp. 8-9; cf. *Letters and Discourses of R. Sandeman*, p. 42.

[2] *Christian Baptist*, edit. 6, pp. 209, 359.

[3] See also *Christian Baptist*, pp. 389, 391, 408, 413, for other instances of the employment of this term in the writings of Sandemanian churches.

[4] *Barnsbury Grove*, p. 7.

[5] Richardson, *Memoirs of A. Campbell*, vol. 2. pp. 125-129.

[6] *Christian Baptist*, edit. 2, Buffalo, Va., 1827, p. 76.

[7] Braidwood's Letters, as cited by Andrew Fuller in his *Strictures on Sandemanianism*, Letter IX.

[8] Richardson, vol. 1. p. 449.

cept or precedent for family worship " in the biblical writings,[1] Mr. Campbell was fortunate enough to discover a justification of the practice in the patriarchal dispensation, which he denominated "the family worship institution;"[2] and, notwithstanding the youthful scruples referred to above, he appears to have performed the duty with a commendable degree of diligence and spirit.

The same people who could not reconcile it to their views to pray or to enjoy any kind of religious observance in the family circle with those who were not in communion with them at the Lord's Supper, yet had no scruples against accompanying respectable persons of whatever creed, or of no creed at all, to the theatre, or against joining with them in the dance or other social amusements which are commonly condemned by the more serious portion of the religious community.[3]

Mr. Campbell was not guilty of this kind of extravagance; but the sentiment of the Sandemanians in the matter of theatres, dancing, and other diversions, appears to have survived in the Mormon community, who, as will be suggested later on, are connected, through the Disciples, with the Sandemanian stock.

It would be natural to expect that those who were unwilling to engage in family prayer where unbelieving members might belong to the household, should also be forward to propose objections to the presence of any but communicants at the public services of the Church. A portion of the Sandemanian Churches acceded to the demand of their peculiar logic in this particular, and were solicitous to exclude from their public worship all who might not belong to their own community.[4]

Mr. Campbell, in his turn, was much taken with this peculiarity of the Sandemanians. His biographer is our authority for the statement that the first church he organized — at Brush Run in Pennsylvania — did not recognize as duly prepared to partake in religious services any persons except such as had professed to put on Christ in baptism; or, in other words, those who chanced to be members of that special organization. Later in life he was persuaded to recede from this extreme position; but he appears to have always regretted his course in that regard, longing in

---

[1] Fuller, *Strictures on Sandemanianism*, Letter IX.

[2] *Christian System*, Bethany, Va., 1840, pp. 128-133

[3] *Barnsbury Grove*, p. 9; compare Fuller's *Strictures on Sandemanianism*, Letter II.; and "Letter of John Glas to Edward Gorril," in *Letters and Discourses of R.S.*, p. 88.

[4] *Christian Baptist*, edit. 6, p. 389; also a "Letter from the Elders of the Church in Dundee to the Elders of the Church in Edinburgh," as found in the *Letters and Discourses of Robert Sandeman*, Dundee, 1851, pp. 116, 117.

vain for the exclusive attitude of his youthful time.[1]

The Sandemanians made a deal of noise over the point that the first day of the week is not properly a Sabbath, at least holding that it is not a duty incumbent upon Christian people to observe it in the same fashion as the Sabbath was observed by the Jewish nation under the Old Testament economy. They regarded the Christian Sabbath as merely designed for the celebration of divine ordinances,[2] and did not conceive that they were engaged to sanctify the day according to the strict usage of the Scottish Kirk. When the concerns of public worship had been duly cared for, the balance of the day might be passed in such pleasures as would scarcely comport with the claim that it was anyway more holy than other days.[3]

The Disciples likewise decline to regard the first day of the week as a Sabbath, or even to call it by that name. The fourth command of the Decalogue, they hold, is applicable to the seventh day, but it does not refer to Sunday. On this account they have now and then been charged with the crime of paying no respect to the Fourth Commandment. Claims of that nature, however, are commonly based upon a misconception. The public worship which the Disciples, like the Sandemanians, consider it their duty to observe on the Lord's Day, occupies about as many hours of time and service as customarily are passed in that way by those who are willing to consider the day as a Sabbath. The only matter worthy of attention in this connection is, that the party are in the habit of proposing the same distinction regarding this subject that was urged, before their time, by the Sandemanians.[4]

---

[1] Richardson, vol. 1, p. 454.

[2] *Barnsbury Grove*, p. 4

[3] Andrew Fuller, *Strictures on Sandemanianism*, Letter IX.

[4] Richardson, vol. 1. pp. 432-435.

CHAPTER III:
"THE ANCIENT GOSPEL"

The main strength and care of the Sandemanian party, during the first twenty-five years of its existence, were exerted in the direction of the constitution, life, and worship of the Church. In the development of these it may be suspected, without any grave lack of charity, that they were influenced, to some extent, by a desire to antagonize the usages of the Kirk of Scotland. The points brought forward in the preceding section will suggest, in several instances, the operation of a spirit of contradiction. For example, the scruple against the propriety of family prayer may have had some kind of reference to the circumstance that this was, at the moment, an almost universal custom of the Scottish country. The tenet against the sanctification of the Sabbath was likewise very offensive to the majority of religious people in Scotland. Historical records are believed to indicate that the custom of observing the Lord's Supper every Sunday had a degree of reference to the circumstance that the Kirk folk commonly celebrated the sacrament but once or twice in the year.

In brief, the Sandemanians were almost always and everywhere in the opposition. This spirit of opposition displayed itself when, in due course of time, they found it desirable to give a portion of their attention to the doctrines which their Church should maintain. The influence of the Methodist movement was by that time beginning to be recognized in Scotland. While the Calvinistic theologians felt impelled to resist the views of Mr. Wesley at various points in the department of soteriology, it is none the less true, that, through the influence of Whitefield, these had gained some degree of currency in the land of Knox. Methodist influences were very much extended in the party of Seceders, who went away from the Established Church in 1732, only a few years after the expulsion of Mr. Glas.

Mr. James Hervey, a member of Wesley's "godly club" at Oxford, who subsequently adhered to the predestinarian views of Whitefield, in the year 1755 had published a work under the title of *"Dialogues between Theron and Aspasio,"* that were received with much popularity. The views that were there set forth regarding the nature of justifying faith and the process of salvation were pretty strongly tinctured with Methodist sentiment, but they were not on that account any the less welcome to wide circles of his readers in Scotland.

Two years later a son-in-law of Mr. Glas — Mr. Robert Sandeman, who likewise had a sort of mission to contend against the "popular preachers" and "popular doctrines" — came forward with a review of the performance of Mr. Hervey, entitled "*Letters on Theron and Aspasio*." In this production he strictly combats the notion advanced by Hervey, that saving faith embraces in its contents any "real persuasion that the blessed Jesus has shed his blood for *me,* or has fulfilled all righteousness in my stead," and also the position that any "appropriation of Christ is essential to faith."[1] What he several times christens as "the ancient gospel,"[2] recognizes as "involved in the contents of justifying faith nothing else than simply believing the record, or crediting the testimony of God."[3] In order to believe the record, Mr. Sandeman wholly discredits the notion that there is a necessity for the operation of the Spirit.[4] He suggests that the Spirit "who breathes in the Scriptures never speaks a word to any man beside what he publicly speaks there;" and he "will not bear to hear the living and powerful Word of God, on any pretense or under color of any distinction whatsoever, called a *dead letter.*"

In the "*Letters on Theron and Aspasio,*" though his tone is extremely bitter and arrogant, he is nevertheless more moderate than he exhibits himself in some of his subsequent productions. The "*Epistolary Correspondence between S. Pike and R. Sandeman*" transcends all the previous limits which he had assigned to his passion. There he claims that faith is "the bare belief of the bare truth," and that it does not even imply so much as a hearty persuasion.

In this bare belief he was also at pains to specify that the mind of the subject is not active, but passive; for, if the mind were active in the matter of crediting the testimony of Christ, this would be the same as to allow that we are justified by an act of the human mind.

Mr. Sandeman, who invented the phrase "ancient gospel," is likewise believed to be the inventor of the very common Disciple phrase, "the good confession,"[5] which several times occurs in the "*Letters on Theron and Aspasio.*"[6] In another part of the same work he gives himself the pains to explain what are the contents of this confession: "There is but one genuine truth that can save men. To illustrate this matter, let it be

---

[1] Sandeman, *Letters on Theron and Aspasio*, New York, 1888, p. 4.
[2] *Ibid.,* p. 117, p. 297, p. 412; *Epistolary Correspondence*, p. 25, p. 83
[3] *Letters*, as above, p. 21.
[4] *Ibid.,* pp. 29-30. [see 1 Timothy 3:15-17; Acts 2:37-38]
[5] [This phrase is found in 1 Timothy 6:12-13.]
[6] *Ibid.,* p. 487.

remembered that the saving truth which the apostles believed was, *That Jesus is the Christ.* The apostles had one uniform fixed sense to these words; and the whole New Testament is written to ascertain to us in what sense they understood them."[1]

Nearly all of these peculiarities come to sight in the theology of the Disciples. Their gospel is commonly denominated "the ancient gospel." In the "*Christian Baptist,*" of which he was the editor, may be found a series of ten different essays from the hand of Mr. Campbell, under that title. The "popular doctrine" and the "popular preachers" are as liberally denounced, and commonly with the same significant expressions, in the pages of that periodical, as in any of the writings of the Sandemanians.

Mr. Campbell is also as clear as his teacher was, that the root and substance of religion is found in knowledge, exclusive of approbation: "evidence alone produces faith, or testimony is all that is necessary to faith."[2] In his "Dialogue between Timothy and Austin," he is believed to come near to the position of Sandeman, that the Spirit never speaks a word to any man besides what he publicly speaks in the Scriptures. Walter Scott, one of his leading assistants, was also a diligent disciple of Sandeman's. In that character he affirms that "the body of Christ is increased by the belief of the bare truth that Jesus is the Son of God and our Saviour."[3]

The distinction which Mr. Sandeman acquired by means of his labors in the department of Christian doctrine was so great, that in a brief season he began to outshine Mr. Glas, who was the founder of the sect. In England and other countries where his writings were circulated, they produced a somewhat violent controversy, in which the name of Glas was but seldom heard. By degrees, therefore, it befell that the adherents of the fraternity came to be known as *Sandemanians* almost everywhere outside of the limits of Scotland; and even there the customary designation has come to be Glasites or Sandemanians, a circumstance which shows that the impression produced by Sandeman was profound and enduring.

It is not important to the purpose in hand, to lay before the reader any detailed account of the literary opponents who entered the lists against the principles that were advanced by Mr. Sandeman. The names of a few of the most prominent will be sufficient to show that he was not neglected. Mr. John Wesley was among the first to come forward with a

---

[1] *Letters* etc., p. 258.
[2] *Christian Baptist*, edit. 6, p. 58.
[3] *Christian Baptist*, edit. 6, p. 21.

brief essay, which he published anonymously as "*A Sufficient Answer to the Author of the Letters on Theron and Aspasio.*" Mr. W. Cudworth, a Dissenting minister of prominence in London, first entered into a private correspondence with Sandeman,[1] and afterwards published a couple of volumes against him. The earliest of these, printed in the year 1760, at London, was entitled "*A Defence of Theron and Aspasio against the Objections contained in a Late Treatise, entitled Letters on Theron and Aspasio.*" The next year appeared "*The Polyglot, or Hope of Eternal Life according to the Various Sentiments of the Present Day.*"

In America, the Rev. Joseph Bellamy, D.D., took part in the conflict with a work entitled, "*Theron, Paulinus, and Aspasio; or, Letters and Dialogues on the Nature of Love to God, Faith in Christ, and Assurance of a Title to Eternal Life,*"[2] as also in the year 1762, with "*An Essay on the Nature and Glory of the Gospel; designed as a Supplement to the Letters and Dialogues.*"

Mr. Isaac Backus likewise gave attention to the issues involved, in a volume published at Boston in 1767, under the title, "*True Faith will produce Good Works. A Discourse wherein are opened the Nature of Faith, and its Powerful Influence on the Heart and Life: together with the Contrary Nature and Effects of Unbelief: and Answers to Various Objections. To which are prefixed, A Brief View of the Present State of the Protestant World, with some Remarks on the Writings of Mr. Sandeman.*"

Some years afterwards, Mr. Andrew Fuller of England was drawn into the controversy by means of an attack upon his position, in the second edition of a work by Mr. Archibald McLean of Edinburgh, entitled "*The Commission of Christ.*" In this treatise, Mr. McLean having set forth some objections to the views of Fuller, the latter replied in an appendix to his book called "*The Gospel Worthy of All Acceptation.*" The answer of Mr. McLean appeared under the title of "*A Reply to Mr. Fuller's Appendix to his Book on the Gospel Worthy of All Acceptation.*" This performance on the part of McLean subsequently called forth Fuller's "*Strictures on Sandemanianism,*" which is, perhaps, the most satisfactory treatment of the whole subject that has yet been published on either side of the question.

---

[1] *Letters and Discourses of R. Sandeman*, p. 37
[2] 1758, 1759

CHAPTER IV:
"THE ANCIENT GOSPEL" IMPROVED

The churches that were under the direction of Sandeman and Glas were making slight progress in different portions of Scotland, when in the year 1761 the faithful were considerably elated by the accession of the Rev. Robert Carmichael, a Seceder minister of the Anti-Burgher type, who presided over a church of that faith at Cupar in Angus.[1]

Carmichael was forthwith assigned to duty in the ranks of the sect to which he had attached his fortunes, and placed in charge of a church in Glasgow. Here it appears that he enjoyed a degree of success; at any rate, he is supposed to have been the means of perverting from his loyalty to the Scottish Kirk, Mr. Archibald McLean, who entered the fraternity of the Sandemanian Independents in the year 1762.[2]

The satisfaction of the Sandemanians with their Anti-Burgher convert was of brief duration. The hand of Mr. Glas was found to be very heavy. Upon the occasion of a case of discipline in which Glas interfered,[3] Carmichael became disgusted with his situation, and laid down the charge of the Independent Church in Glasgow.[4] Archibald McLean, apparently a *protégé* of Carmichael's, also retired from the sect on the same occasion.[5]

After this pair of friends had fallen into a condition of separation from the Sandemanians, it was not singular that they should have qualms of conscience touching some of the tenets that were maintained by that fraternity. In this instance criticism was leveled against the doctrine of infant-baptism, which Mr. Glas had retained as a prominent item of the "ancient order of things."[6] As a natural consequence, both of them in due season renounced the practice of infant-baptism.

Carmichael speedily removed from Glasgow to Edinburgh, where he seems to have had charge of an Independent Church that had likely seceded from the community over which Mr. Robert Sandeman was then presiding in that city; it is believed to have been composed of people

---

[1] *Letters and Discourses of Robert Sandeman*, p. 44, p. 93; cf. also *Memoir of Archibald McLean,* by William Jones, p. xxiii. This memoir is printed in front of the first volume of McLean's collected works, published at Elgin, Scotland, 1847.

[2] *Memoir of McLean*, pp. xxii.

[3] *Letters and Discourses*, p. 83

[4] *Letters and Discourses,* p. 44, note.

[5] *Memoir*, p. xxiii.

[6] *Memoir*, p. xxiii.

who took the part of Carmichael in the controversy that he had waged with Glas and Sandeman in Glasgow. They were only seven in number, but they invited Carmichael from Glasgow to be their pastor.[1]

As he was on the point of setting out for Edinburgh, Mr. McLean promised his old pastor that he would compose a letter, in which should be laid down in full his views on the subject of baptism. When this document was completed, it was dated on the 2nd of July, 1764. Mr. Carmichael obtained it by due course of mail; but as he was now comfortably established in Edinburgh, over a church that was still in doctrinal agreement with Mr. Sandeman, he was uncertain what might be the result in case he should suddenly profess his conversion to the views of those who opposed infant-baptism. It was more than possible that his adherents would refuse to give attention to his reasons; they might even dismiss him on the spot, and return to the community from which they had but recently taken their leave. Consequently Mr. Carmichael, who is suspected to have been devoid of any thing like stability of character, still persisted in the practice of baptizing infants.[2]

After the lapse of a twelve months, however, Carmichael had succeeded in convincing five of his seven parishioners of the unlawfulness of infant-baptism, and of the propriety of immersion as the act of baptism. Apparently by their vote or consent, he was dispatched to London for the purpose of obtaining immersion at the hands of some of the Baptist ministers of England. He was immersed at the baptistery in the Barbican, by Dr. John Gill, on the 9th of October, 1765. On his return to Edinburgh, he in his turn immersed the five persons who had consorted with him, and two others; thus laying the foundations of the Sandemanian Church of the immersion observance, who are otherwise designated by the name of "Scotch Baptists."[3] The Sandemanians of the aspersion[4] observance, under the lead of Sandeman and Glas, were in the custom of expressing their disgust against this unwelcome conduct on the part of a portion of their adherents, by denouncing the same as Anabaptists.[5]

After a few weeks, McLean drew nigh from Glasgow, and caused himself to be immersed. In the month of July 1767, he went to London

---

[1] *Memoirs of McLean*, p. xxiii.
[2] *Memoirs of McLean*, pp. xxiii and xxiv.
[3] *Memoirs*, p. xxiv.
[4] [Pouring or sprinkling]
[5] *Letters and Discourses of Robert Sandeman*, Dundee, 1851, p. 48, note.

for the purpose of trying his fortunes as a printer;[1] but failing to meet with such a degree of encouragement as he desired, he accepted a position in Edinburgh which brought him into immediate contact with Carmichael and the immersed Sandemanians of that place. He entered Edinburgh in December 1767; in June 1768, he was raised from his station as a private member, to the dignity of fellow-elder with Carmichael.[2] Although there were only nine members in the community,[3] Sandemanian literalism was very strenuous to require that they should maintain a plurality of elders.

It was only a brief season before Carmichael found it convenient to quit the immersed Sandemanians, and to return to the Sandemanians of the aspersion observance; in the year 1773, he was presiding over such a church in Edinburgh.[4] It was perhaps the same church which Robert Sandeman left behind when he came to America in the year 1764.[5] The founder of the so-called "Scotch Baptists " was, therefore, one of the first to leave the church which he had established; it is suspected that his convictions were either not very strong or not very sincere. By the defection of Carmichael, Mr. McLean was immediately recognized as the undisputed leader of the immersed Sandemanians.

McLean had not been long installed in his position at Edinburgh before his mind was persuaded that it would be a feasible enterprise to make some improvements upon "the ancient gospel," as invented by the philosophy of Mr. Sandeman. The latter gentleman appeared to consider that he was set to oppose every prominent tenet that had come to be advocated by the Seceders or by others, who, within the limits of Scotland or elsewhere, had in any way been influenced by the progress of the Wesleyan revival. While the Westminster Confession had inculcated[6] the doctrine of assurance of faith, it had been studious to avoid including that grace in the contents of saving faith. On the contrary, it expressly provides "that this infallible assurance doth not so belong to the essence of faith, but that a true believer may wait long, and conflict with many difficulties, before he be partaker of it; yet, being enabled by the Spirit to know the things which are freely given him of God, he may, without extraordinary revelation, in the right use of ordinary means, attain

---

[1] *Memoirs*, p. xix

[2] *Memoirs*, pp. xxiv, xxi, xxv.

[3] Benedict, ed. 2, p. 355

[4] *Memoir of Mr. William Braidwood*, p. xvii.

[5] "Biography of Sandeman," prefixed to his *Discourses*, Dundee, 1857, p. xi.

[6] [Taught.]

thereunto."[1]

The Seceders and many others, including some of the more zealous pastors within the Established Church, had now begun to reckon a fixed assurance of one's personal acceptance as belonging among the invariable elements of saving faith. Sandeman naturally took umbrage against this innovation on the part of the "popular preachers;" and, in keeping with his character and position, he was soon found at the opposite extreme, not only denying that assurance is of the essence of saving faith, but also affirming that the Christian could never attain to any better estate in this world than an assurance of *the possibility* of his personal salvation. He understands the ancient gospel to be that "divine truth which affords hope to the vilest transgressor, that he *may be justified*, that he *may escape* the curse."[2] Sandeman likewise adds[3] that "the simple belief of the gospel" (which, according to him, is all that faith implies or embraces) "leaves a man, even in the full assurance of faith, or when the truth is most present to his thoughts, entirely at the mercy of God for salvation, and leads him to the greatest reverence for, and submission to, the Divine sovereignty, without having any claim upon God whatsoever, or finding any reason why God should regard him more than those who perish."

Mr. McLean was not well content with this comfortless view of his master. Accordingly, in the work on the *"Commission of Jesus Christ,"* already mentioned, while he continues to accept Sandeman's conceit about the nature of evangelical faith,[4] he demurs to the conclusion that "the bare belief of the bare truth" will do nothing more than Sandeman affirmed for the benefit of the individual subject, and assumes the ground that this bare belief is just as capable of conveying the immediate assurance of salvation as was the saving faith advocated by the most ardent Seceder.[5]

The hyper-Calvinist opinions of Sandeman were likewise no longer acceptable to McLean, seeing that they were employed not as ordinarily to confirm the assurance of the faithful, but on the contrary to prevent

---

[1] chap, xviii. sec. 3 [It is incredible that the author of this book appeals to the Westminster Confession of Faith as the authority, instead of the Bible, showing his faith comes from man, and not God.—*Editor.*]

[2] *Letter on Theron and Aspasio,* N.Y., 1838, p. 290; cf. McLean's *Commission of Jesus Christ,* Edinburgh, 1786, p. 96, footnote.

[3] *Ibid.,* p. 295.

[4] *Commission of Jesus Christ,* p. 80.

[5] *Commission,* pp. 90-98.

them from cherishing any stronger faith than that which affirms a possibility that the most devout and correct of them *may be justified.* That was, indeed, a distressing prospect which others besides McLean — persons who stood much nearer to the master — were pained to accept.

From considerations of this kind the leader of the immersed wing of the Sandemanian fraternity appears to have conceived a certain distaste for the extreme views regarding the Calvinistic system of truth, which prevailed in the opposing camp. He was, therefore, able to content himself with a somewhat moderate position in relation to questions of that nature.

Professing to hold in good esteem the bare belief by means of which Sandeman had relegated the origin of personal religion to the sphere of the intellect, excluding any right operations of the emotions or of the will, he was nevertheless, as a matter of fact, unable to obtain a very high degree of confidence in the efficacy of an agent that was so attenuated.[1] The assurance which this mere belief might be competent to bestow was dried up, indeed, as the best article in that line which was then offered to the favor of the "professing world;" but flaming commendations of this kind had long since become familiar, and they were generally estimated at their proper value.

In order, therefore, to improve his emasculated faith, — "to make assurance double sure, and take a bond of fate," — McLean resolved to provide this mere intellectual exercise with a buttress that was designed to support its weakness and secure its existence. This buttress consisted of an addition to the design of baptism, which necessarily had escaped the attention of the party which continued in the practice of infant-baptism. What *it* could not do, in that it was weak, it was hoped might be performed by the immersion of believers in water. Accordingly Mr. McLean advances the peculiar theory of baptism for the remission of sins.[2] Baptism was clearly asserted to be necessary to salvation;[3] not in the way of baptismal regeneration, however, but in the way of effecting the remission of sins after the act of mere belief.

Another feature of Mr. McLean's teaching on the subject of baptism is found in the fact that he insisted that it should be performed, not "in the name of the Father, Son, and Holy Ghost," as is the custom of the balance of the Christian world, but on the contrary "*into* the name, etc."[4]

---

[1] [Weakened]

[2] *Commission of Jesus Christ,* Edinburgh, 1786, pp. 129-137. [See Acts 2:38]

[3] *Ibid.,* pp. 131-132 [see 1 Peter 3:21; Mark 16:16]

[4] *Commission,* pp. 110-114 [See Matthew 28:19, ASV]

He likewise maintains in the same connection,[1] that "the Holy Spirit was not given, in a way peculiar to the gospel dispensation, during John's baptism, nor till Christ was glorified."

Each of the peculiarities above described has been reproduced by the Disciples (or *Campbellites*) in America. They reject infant baptism; they practice immersion exclusively for baptism; they hold the necessity of baptism for the remission of sins, urging the very same passages of Scripture, and in the same way, as Archibald McLean, in support of that notion; they insist upon the propriety of baptizing "*into* the name of the Father, Son, and Holy Spirit;" and they declare that the kingdom of heaven was not completely set up until the Day of Pentecost. If the above were not matters of common fame, it would be in order to produce citations from their literature in each case; but, as nobody will think or care to call in question the fact that these things are now customary in the ranks of the Disciples, it may not be necessary to bring forward any such special proofs of the statements here advanced.

---

[1] *Ibid.*, p. 113.

CHAPTER V:
THE HALDANEANS

The tide of religious revival flowed so strongly in Scotland, that at length, just before the close of the eighteenth century, it reached the ranks of the laity also. These now began to experience an amount of confidence and zeal which was sufficient to induce them to go forward in Christian labor, and in some instances even to assume the functions, and to invade the prerogatives of the regular clergy. The most prominent in this somewhat notable movement were the brothers Robert and James Alexander Haldane. They were of gentle birth and breeding. Robert, who was the elder, had in possession an estate which, according to the standard then prevalent in Scotland, was regarded as highly respectable.

On the 6th of May 1797, nearly two and twenty years after the establishment of the first society of "Scotch Baptists" or immersed Sandemanians, the tongue of James Alexander Haldane was loosed. He delivered his maiden discourse to a company of colliers at the village of Gilmerton, in the vicinity of Edinburgh. His social position, combined with his previous experience of life, and his remarkable abilities in the line of popular preaching, imparted a high degree of interest and importance to this event.[1]

James Alexander Haldane followed the sea in his earlier years, where he had attained the dignity of captain in the merchant marine, and only a short while previously had resigned command of the ship "Melville Castle," that was engaged in the East-India service.[2] After his introduction to the work of lay-preaching at Gilmerton, Mr. Haldane was seized with an unwonted degree of religious fervor and pious solicitude. A little more than two months from that date, on the 12th of July, he set forward on a missionary journey to the Highlands of Scotland, which was rewarded with so large a share of encouragement and success, that, before it was concluded on the 7th of November 1797, his name and his enterprise were the occasion of general remark.

Events now fell out with much rapidity in the progress of the revival. Instead of remaining quietly in the bosom of the Kirk, where was ample room for them, and many gave their sympathy, the Haldane brothers were soon taking steps which looked in the direction of a secession from

---

[1] *Memoirs of Robert and James Alexander Haldane,* by Alexander Haldane, Esq., New York, 1853, pp. 140-141.

[2] *Memoirs,* as above, p. 74.

that institution. On the 11th of January, 1798, was formed by them and such of their friends as would allow their names to be used in that relation, a "Society for Propagating the Gospel at Home."[1] A single year was space enough, after this step had been performed, for the movement to develop into a church organization. In January 1799, the first Haldanean society was constituted at Edinburgh, and on the 3rd of February they publicly ordained James A. Haldane to be their pastor.[2]

The public are familiar with the marvels that were accomplished by the promoters of this enterprise in the period between the years 1797 and 1808, as likewise with the lamentable declension which then set in and almost in a day destroyed its usefulness and promise.

The causes of that unhappy catastrophe are pretty clearly suggested in the biography of the Haldanes already cited; by the aid of the light which is there supplied, it is possible to trace the operation of these causes from stage to stage in the downward course. At the very beginning of the undertaking, James A. Haldane chanced to be on an intimate footing with a certain Dr. Charles Stuart of Dunearn.[3] This gentleman was likewise of noble blood, of excellent learning, many attractive social qualities, and of the queerest kind of a head. He had begun life as a minister in the Established Kirk. After his accession to the parish of Cramond, near Edinburgh, he was united in marriage to a daughter of the venerable John Erskine, the leader of the evangelical wing in that institution;[4] but he was not appointed to pursue his career in peace and usefulness. The biographer of the Haldanes[5] declares that "in his thirst for general information and the society of good men, Dr. Stuart had gone from the Divinity Hall in Edinburgh, to some of the Dissenting Academies in London, and there imbibed notions unfavorable to the union between Church and State." Whatever may be the fact regarding his visits to London, the notions which he entertained and propagated on that topic were to be had much nearer home; they were the leading article of the Independents, or Sandemanians, and might be read any day in the *"Testimony of the King of Martyrs,"* the principal work of Mr. John Glas. It was published in Edinburgh, just under the nose of Dr. Stuart, and was kept on sale in most of the booksellers' shops of the country.

More than this, Dr. Stuart had acquired convictions against the pro-

---

[1] *Memoirs*, pp. 178-179.
[2] *Memoirs*, p. 217.
[3] *Memoirs*, p. 140.
[4] *Memoirs*, pp. 125-126.
[5] p. 141.

priety of the practice of infant-baptism and against the mode of baptism by aspersion; and at the moment when he conceived his perhaps interested admiration for James A. Haldane, he was duly numbered in the lists of the "Scotch Baptists," or Sandemanians of the immersion observance;[1] and was a member of Archibald McLean's Church.[2]

When James A. Haldane preached his first sermon in the evening of the 6th of May 1797, this ardent and excellent "Scotch Baptist" was present to applaud the effort. He seems almost upon the spot to have conceived the ambition to make a proselyte of his friend. He declared that to see him a Baptist would be the consummation of his earthly felicity. He "took much pains to inculcate Baptist views upon Haldane, attended his ministry, listened to his preaching with rapt admiration, and called on him two or three times in every week to discuss the topics which were delivered from the pulpit." No art or blandishment of the determined and skillful proselytizer was neglected. It is with justice that the biographer admits,[3] "There is no doubt that Dr. Stuart's influence on Mr. James Haldane was considerable, as it was also on several other eminent men." In sad truth this excellent, wrong-headed gentleman was the evil genius of the Haldanes and of their cause. Had they at the outset possessed a sufficient amount of insight and foresight to have bestowed upon him a firm and enduring repulse, they might have escaped the shipwreck which shortly stranded themselves and their movement on the shallows of Sandemanian literalism.

We are given to understand that there were "several other eminent men" over whom Dr. Stuart exerted a degree of injurious influence. Notable among these was Mr. Greville Ewing, one of the leading co-adjutors[4] of the Haldanes. Already before the year 1795 there were possibly some relations of intimacy between Stuart and Ewing, for in that year we find the latter advocating the practice of "mutual exhortation" from the pulpit of Lady Glenorchy's chapel in Edinburgh, where he was assistant to the Rev. Dr. Jones.[5] Mr. Ewing likewise declares elsewhere in the same work.[6] that the origin of his dissatisfaction with the

---

[1] *Memoirs*, pp. 141, 338, and 511-512

[2] *Memoirs of William Braidwood*, p. 36, note.

[3] *Memoirs...Haldane*, p. 141

[4] [Co-workers.]

[5] *Facts and Documents respecting the Connections which have subsisted between Robert Haldane, Esq., and Greville Ewing. By Greville Ewing.* Glasgow 1809, pp. 127-128, note.

[6] *Ibid.*, p. 8.

Church of Scotland, of which he was a minister, "was the exercise of a power by church courts over ministers and congregations, which restrained the former from preaching wherever they had an opportunity, and the latter from adopting any plan for mutual edification and comfort," — a kind of scruple which, in the latter instance, has a decided odor of Dr. Stuart and the Sandemanians.

In the year 1796, a twelve month before the project of the Haldanes was mooted, the celebrated "Missionary Magazine" was commenced "under the auspices of Dr. Stuart, with Mr. Ewing as editor."[1] A connection of this kind, in which an active and prominent minister of the Kirk allowed himself to become, in a certain sort, the spokesman, if not the creature, of a leading character among the "Scotch Baptists," could not fail to excite remark and to give offense. It was, therefore, in no way singular that Mr. Ewing's position in the Establishment should every day become more untenable.[2] In the progress of time and instruction, his conversion to the practices and tenets of the immersed Sandemanians might have become as complete and extensive as that of the brothers Haldane subsequently was, if the relation with Stuart had not been early broken off by changes which will be mentioned in their place farther on. The "Missionary Magazine" was not infrequently supplied with articles which suggested that the editor was making fair advances in the doctrines of the proprietor.[3]

When it is brought to mind that this same "Missionary Magazine," "under the auspices of Dr. Stuart," and whose editor was, after a fashion, his disciple, became from the beginning the official organ of the Haldanean enterprise, it will be apparent how large a hold the immersed wing of the Sandemanian sect had acquired upon the fortunes and the future of a promising cause. To some minds it may seem a fair conclusion that it was never possible for the new church to have attained permanent success. Too many elements, which could signify no other fate than early disaster, were present at its inception. None of the least of these may be perceived in the circumstance that when, in the month of December 1798, the project of founding a church was broached, Mr. Ewing, "as being most familiar with such matters, was requested to draw up a plan for its government."[4]

For a season after the inauguration of the earliest church, in January

---

[1] *Memoirs*, p. 141.
[2] *Memoirs*, p. 179.
[3] *Memoirs*, p. 214.
[4] *Memoirs*, p. 214.

1799, the best wishes of the Haldanes were fulfilled; but it was a sadly brief season.

The storms which they had not the wisdom and experience to fore-cast speedily began to gather about their heads. As soon as Mr. Ewing had seceded from the Church of Scotland, he placed himself at the service of Robert Haldane to be employed in forwarding the plans that gentleman had in mind. Mr. Haldane had made arrangements to send a class of students to Gosport, England, where they might remain for a time under the care of the well-known Dr. Bogue, as a means of preparing them for the work of the ministry. But it was given to Mr. Ewing to persuade his friend that it would be wiser to commit these students to his own care, since there were somewhat decided objections against Dr. Bogue in Scotland, and perhaps elsewhere, on the score of his liberal politics. On the 2nd of January 1799, Greville Ewing opened his seminary of theology in Edinburgh. The number of pupils at first was twenty-four, derived from various denominations, except the Congregationalists or Sandemanians; but before the course was ended, one of their number affirms that they all found themselves decided and intelligent Congregationalists.[1] This was a marked degree of success. Few men are to be found who had a surer command of the arts of proselytizing than Mr. Ewing.

Yet there were reasons why Robert Haldane should not be highly elated by the triumphs of his subordinate. Mr. Ewing was much addicted to the writings of Glas and Sandeman; but at this particular period of his career Mr. Haldane was less favorably inclined towards those theologians than he subsequently came to be, through the unhappy influence of Dr. Stuart upon the mind of James A. Haldane. Accordingly, when Ewing put the books that have been referred to in the hands of the students,[2] Mr. Haldane considered he was entitled to interpose, which step he took immediately, while Ewing and the students were still in the city of Edinburgh.[3] This must have been the beginning of the troubles which for so many years wasted the strength and spirits of the two men, and ultimately brought calamities on the cause they had engaged to promote.

When his attention was first directed to the danger that existed in Edinburgh, Robert Haldane assumed a wise position. If he had but pressed forward vigorously in the sentiments which he then entertained, he might have rescued his interests from ruin. He was opposed even to

---

[1] *Memoirs*, p. 228.
[2] *Facts and Documents*, p. 79, cf. p. 82.
[3] *Facts and Documents*, pp. 134-135.

the notions of Church order inculcated by Glas and Sandeman, as well as to their "ancient gospel;"[1] but on this side of the subject his sentiments later underwent an unhappy modification,[2] and he embraced with decision, and in some cases with passion, a great many items of the desolating scheme of the Sandemanians.

There was a curious play of cross purposes in this business. After the unpleasantness which occurred at Edinburgh, Mr. Ewing seemed to consider it the main concern of his existence to find a place in every question which should be on the opposite side from that which Robert Haldane was led to assume. Therefore, at the moment when Haldane in his turn began to dabble considerably in the "ancient order of things," Ewing was beginning to insist on occupying the old ground. Yet, notwithstanding all the counsel which he had brought himself to accept from Glas and Sandeman in the details of Church order, Robert Haldane could never prevail upon himself to receive as true what they had inculcated regarding the nature of saving faith. Observing this peculiarity, Ewing, always in the opposition, became more and more attached to the Sandemanian notion that faith is nothing else than bare belief.

According to the legally formulated terms of an arrangement that had been fixed upon already before he was given charge of the students, Ewing removed to Glasgow at Whitsunday 1799, to take the pastoral oversight of a church which he was expected to organize in the Circus, a large building there which Robert Haldane had recently purchased for three thousand pounds, and fitted up for the purpose of religious worship. The seminary was also removed with him. Confidence between the two men being now to a large extent destroyed, it was the earnest desire of Ewing to become entirely independent of Mr. Haldane,[3] by securing the Circus building for himself and for the people who should join his society. He hoped to effect this purpose by inducing Haldane to make over the house to his people in the way of a gift; but the latter was not in the least disposed to accede to that proposal. Ewing persisted for a number of years, always becoming more and more embittered and unreasonable, until at last both parties appeared before the public in volumes of abusive charges directed against each other. But the difference is believed to have started from nothing else than a contrariety of opinions regarding the merits of the Sandemanians. Except for this issue the two might have passed their whole lives without a word of conflict.

---

[1] *Facts and Documents*, pp. 134-135.

[2] *Facts and Documents*, p. 81.

[3] *Facts and Documents*, p. 24.

Not in the least willing to respect the wishes of Haldane, Mr. Ewing, after his removal to the West, still kept the writings of Glas and Sandeman prominently before his students. Robert Haldane was much chafed by that usage. When James A. Haldane went to Dumfries in the summer of the year 1801, being now at a distance from Edinburgh and from his brother, he wrote Ewing a letter which had possibly been suggested before he left home, warning him against the retention of these books in the seminary, and complaining of his enthusiastic manner of speaking of those frigid and bitter theologians.[1] This resource, which was perhaps immediately suspected, did not in the least avail: Ewing kept on his way. At last, in the year 1802, hopeless of his ability to reduce him to terms by any other means, Robert Haldane incontinently removed the seminary from Glasgow back to Edinburgh, and placed it in other hands.[2] When the institution was opened in the latter place, Mr. Haldane not only forbade the books of Glas and Sandeman in the library, but laid upon the students an express prohibition against reading them anywhere else.[3]

But the time was far past for such precautions. Sandemanian principles were already too deeply established in the minds of his people to admit of their successful eviction by that or by any other method. Dr. Stuart, especially, was whispering them into the ear of James A. Haldane in two or three private interviews every week; and Robert Haldane himself appears after a few years, through the influence of his brother, to perform the role of an exceedingly tenacious stickler for some of the most fantastic features of the "ancient order of things."[4] In this regard he outstripped Mr. Ewing by many degrees, and sometimes sorely harassed the consciences of his adherents; but in regard to the nature of faith, Ewing was much in the lead of both the brothers.

When, in the summer of the year 1800, Mr. Ewing at length, on the occasion of a temporary truce with Haldane[5] got the consent of his mind to organize a church among the people who attended upon his ministry at Glasgow, he issued a handbill for the instruction of his congregation and of the public, entitled "Regulations of the Church, Jamaica Street," in which were included two items of the "ancient order;" namely, the mutual exhortation of the members of the Church, and the weekly celebra-

---

[1] *Memoirs*, pp. 321-322.
[2] *Memoirs*, pp. 299-300.
[3] *Facts and Documents*, p. 82.
[4] *Facts and Documents*, pp. 93-95; *Memoirs*, pp. 322-327.
[5] *Facts and Documents*, pp. 58-64

tion of the Lord's Supper. With regard to the former of these, however, the document seems to indicate that it was to be held not on Sunday, but upon some other day of the week. It is also strict to insist upon what must have been a highly necessary provision: "that no personal remarks, or injurious reports respecting character, were to be allowed in the Church."[1]

The custom of "mutual exhortation," the absence of which from the Scottish Kirk had given him an amount of uneasiness, had likewise been duly introduced by Mr. Ewing into the constitution of the Edinburgh society in December 1798.[2] But the Church in Edinburgh gave no practical heed to that portion of their ecclesiastical chart until a later period, when the practice was inaugurated with a degree of success that was disgusting even to such a standing advocate of "primitive Christianity" as Dr. Stuart himself.[3] On the other hand, the custom of weekly communion was not introduced by Mr. Ewing at the outset into the constitution which he had drawn up for the use of the Edinburgh society, since it was for several years the habit of that body to celebrate the Lord's Supper only once in the month.[4] When, however, the improved example of the Glasgow Church became known to the disciples in Edinburgh, they likewise soon began to break the loaf every Sunday.

But the Haldanes were not prepared to stop at this point. James Haldane, being constantly in receipt of new light from Dr. Stuart and other Sandemanian sources, could not abide that his brilliancy should be concealed under a bushel. Accordingly, in the year 1805, he sent forth the first edition of his "*View of the Social Worship and Ordinances*," the second edition of which has just been cited above. There it is evident that he had made decided progress in the lore of the Sandemanians. Their dialect is in very fine flow upon his pen. He stands forth like a man for the "express precept or approved precedent," about which Thomas Campbell was to speak with so much pathos a few years later in the wilds of Pennsylvania. There should be no creed nor confession of faith but the Scriptures. Here was the first distinct demand for a presbytery with a plurality of elders, that had been openly uttered in the Haldanean con-

---

[1] *Facts and Documents*, pp. 64-65.

[2] "Address by James A. Haldane to the Church of Christ, Leith Walk, Edinburgh." Edinburgh 1808, p. 11. This address is bound up at the back of Mr. Haldane's volume entitled "*A View of the Social Worship and Ordinances of the First Christians*," Edinburgh 1806.

[3] *Memoirs*, p. 340.

[4] *Facts and Documents*, p. 129.

nection. The collection that was always customary at the Lord's Supper now became designated as "the fellowship," after the best approved Sandemanian fashion.

But what gave Mr. Ewing particular offense was the circumstance that "mutual exhortation," which he had confined to Wednesday evening, was raised by Haldane to the dignity of a divine ordinance, and assigned to a place among the regular Sunday observances of the congregation. Thereupon he began to draw back, and went so far the other way, that, in the end, he was seriously accused of entirely deserting his darling innovation.[1] Matters finally got to such a pass that apparently almost the only principle upon which the two parties were heartily at one related to the rejection of creeds. Though they were daily pleading for a union on the Bible, by some kind of means they were daily receding farther from each other, while each faction was accusing the other of a passion for change.

Unhappily for all concerned, Robert Haldane was too much impressed by a sense of the correctness and importance of the Sandemanian notions that had been propounded in his brother's recent publication. James had not expected or desired to produce any immediate results beyond "inciting his brethren in Christ to study the Scriptures on this and every other subject, and to appeal only to the law and to the testimony."[2] But shortly after the book left the press in June 1805, Robert Haldane and Mr. Ballantyne were on a visit to England; and, stopping on their way at Newcastle, they remained for some time practicing the views of social worship that were developed in it.[3] Their conduct in this regard gave much offense.[4] Ballantyne and Haldane, while not excluding those who were not of their own party, publicly exhorted one another in the forenoons, and mutually dispensed the Lord's Supper, without directing their remarks in the least to the audience who had assembled for worship, while in the afternoons and evenings they preached to the multitudes as usual.[5]

No person was bold enough to express the dissatisfaction which many felt against the conduct of the Haldanes, until the year 1807, when Ballantyne issued a *"Treatise on the Elder's Office,"* in which the position of James Haldane and the Sandemanians was duly enforced re-

---

[1] *Facts and Documents*, pp. 126-129.
[2] *View of the Social Worship and Ordinances,* Preface, p. vii.
[3] *Memoirs*, p. 324.
[4] *Memoirs*, p. 327.
[5] *Facts and Documents*, p. 248.

garding the necessity of a plurality of these functionaries to the existence of a gospel Church. There is rarely anything sadder to witness than the spectacle of Robert Haldane, unquestionably a splendid mind and spirit, leading the way in the puerile figures of the dance which John Glas had instructed his own followers. Mr. Haldane became, in an offensive sense, responsible for the work of Ballantyne,[1] doing everything that lay in his power to give it countenance and circulation.

In answer to the challenge which he conceived had by this means been laid upon his own wing of the party, Mr. Ewing forthwith prepared and published an *"Attempt towards a Statement of the Doctrine of Scripture on some disputed points respecting the Constitution, Government, Worship, and Discipline of the Church of Christ,"* Glasgow 1808. The breach between the factions was now first made public: it had long been incurable. The party of Ewing, which, perhaps, was numerically the smaller, became henceforth practically isolated; but their sentiments on the subjects of faith, infant-baptism, the mode of baptism, the duty of weekly communion and of mutual exhortation, placed them in closer sympathy and relations with the Sandemanians of the aspersion observance. On the other hand, the Haldanes were now become, in a measure, reckless. In order that the Edinburgh Church might conform to the apostolic model in the matter of a plurality of elders, Robert was speedily ordained to occupy a place by the side of James Alexander in that function.[2]

Possibly it was not without reference to the circumstance that Mr. Ewing was leaning far to the side of the Sandemanian Independents, that James Haldane now began to turn towards the "Scotch Baptists." The patient labors of Charles Stuart were about to be crowned with success. This consummation was promoted by the action of Mr. John Campbell, a beloved associate of the Haldanes, who had gone over to the "Scotch Baptist" fraternity as early as the year 1803, since which time he had been pastor of a church at Kingsland, near London.[3] In a letter to this gentleman under date of Feb. 19, 1808, Haldane expresses strong scruples regarding the propriety of infant-baptism.[4] The 21st of April, 1808, was the date of another communication which announced that he had been immersed.[5] In a few months Robert also followed his brother in

---

[1] *Facts and Documents,* pp. 97-98

[2] *Memoirs,* p. 341.

[3] *Memoirs,* p. 297.

[4] *Memoirs,* p. 325.

[5] *Memoirs,* p. 325.

these changes.

This action did not result in any kind of organic union between the Haldanians and the party that was led by Mr. Archibald McLean, but it was not many weeks until it had produced a hopeless disruption of the Edinburgh Church and of the entire Haldanean body. The enterprise which started forth with so much promise was brought to hopeless desolation. There has been scarcely anywhere in modern Church history a more lame and impotent conclusion.

The Sandemanians had ruined the cause and Church of the Haldanes.

CHAPTER VI:
MR. CAMPBELL'S PERVERSION TO SANDEMANIANISM (First Stage)

It was not easy to follow in detail the process of Mr. Campbell's perversion to Sandemanian views, until the publication of his biography by Professor Robert Richardson, an early disciple and for many years a bosom friend of the most prominent advocate of Sandemanianism in America. Though we are indebted to his *"Memoirs of Alexander Campbell,"* Philadelphia 1868, for a considerable amount and variety of information regarding the early years of his master, there are still certain points of inquiry where he unhappily leaves us in the lurch. But the occasions for complaint are less numerous than the reasons for gratitude. The account which is here given is based almost entirely upon the representations made by Professor Richardson.

Alexander Campbell was born near Ballymena, County Antrim, Ireland, on the 12th of September, 1788.[1] His father, Thomas Campbell, was a Seceder minister of the Anti-Burgher branch,[2] and lived in quite humble circumstances. After suffering the ills of a probationer's existence for about ten years, his patience was at length rewarded by the pastoral charge of a new church at Ahorey, near Armagh.[3] With the hope of eking out an insufficient salary, the young pastor took a farm near the village of Rich Hill, where he fixed his residence.[4] The farm proving a failure, he went back to his early occupation of teaching school,[5] removing for this purpose into the village. As his family increased in number, the individual advantages of the several children were in a corresponding degree curtailed. Alexander got what education he might at hap-hazard;[6] but for several years, owing to the loss of most of his studious inclinations, his powers went to waste. At length his attention was directed to the importance of cultivation, and he set about the business of self-education,[7] but with no unusual amount of success. Most of the time was passed in the capacity of an assistant in his father's

---

[1] *Memoirs of Alexander Campbell,*, vol. 1. p. 19.

[2] *Ibid.,* vol. 1. p 25.

[3] *Ibid.,* vol. 1. pp. 29-30

[4] *Ibid.,* vol. 1. p. 30.

[5] *Ibid.,* vol. 1. p. 47.

[6] *Ibid.,* vol. 1. pp. 31-35, 48

[7] *Ibid.,* vol. 1. p. 76

school at Rich Hill, or in the performance of similar labors at the school of one of his uncles at Newry.[1]

The circumstances of the family became at length so much straitened that they began to turn their eyes to the United States for "deliverance."[2] The father preceded the balance of the household, setting sail from Londonderry on the 8th of April, 1807.[3] In the course of time he was enabled to provide means for their passage; and they took ship to follow him, on the 1st of October, 1808.[4] The funds for this purpose were likely procured by means of public contributions obtained from the different Presbyterian Churches of Western Pennsylvania.[5]

Six days after their embarkation, the family were wrecked on the island of Islay on the coast of Scotland. Mrs. Campbell, his mother, being unwilling to entrust herself to the hazards of an ocean voyage in the winter season of the year, and Alexander being naturally desirous to repair in some measure the defects of his early education, it was arranged that they should pass the time until the approaching spring should open upon them, at Glasgow, where he might employ his leisure in attending the university. Meanwhile Thomas Campbell was actively engaged at his home in Washington County, Penn., in trying to relieve their distresses, and, in due time, to procure their transfer to the country of his adoption.

Already in their home at Rich Hill, Ireland, they had become familiar with the Scottish Independents. A somewhat flourishing Church of the Glasites, or Sandemanians of the aspersion observance, existed there.[6] Professor Richardson admits[7] that "the Independents exerted a most important influence upon the religious views of both Thomas Campbell and his son Alexander;" but this influence did not become apparent during the period of their residence at Rich Hill. The former, it is true, had much pleasure in attending the religious services of the Sandemanian Church; but he was all the while in the full odor of Seceder orthodoxy, and it is not likely that he would ever have forsaken his own people but for the somewhat extraordinary experiences that he was now

---

[1] *Ibid.,* vol. 1. p. 88

[2] *Ibid.,* vol. 1. pp. 80-81, 86.

[3] *Ibid.,* vol. 1. p. 81.

[4] *Ibid.,* vol. 1. p. 95.

[5] *Debate on Campbellism,* between Alexander Campbell and Obadiah Jennings, Pittsburg 1832, pp. 246-247; compare Richardson, vol. 1. pp. 306-307.

[6] *Memoirs of Campbell,* vol. 1. pp. 60, 82

[7] *Ibid.,* vol. 1. p. 59

called to encounter. Even the membership he held in the Haldanean "Society for Propagating the Gospel at Home"[1] does not necessarily signify any lack of devotion to his lifelong connections in the Presbyterian body. Many persons in various portions of the country had yielded to the eloquent and impassioned solicitations of James A. Haldane so far as to permit themselves to be enrolled in that organization, who had no thought or wish to be known as followers of the Haldanes.

The only perceptible influence exerted by the Sandemanians of Rich Hill upon the Presbyterian pastor of the place may be observed in the fact that he is reported to have made an overture either before the Presbytery of Market Hill or the Synod of Ireland, "in favor of a more frequent celebration of the Lord's Supper;"[2] but it is not stated that he was bold enough to advocate a weekly observance. For the rest, he must have been at this time almost unaffected by the ordinary Sandemanian considerations in favor of the "mutual exhortation" of church members, or of the various other preposterous imitations of Christ that were peculiar to the people in question. In brief, Alexander is believed to have been the leader in the unhappy progress that was later made by both father and son in the direction of the Independents.

When they were wrecked on the island of Islay, one of the most influential persons with whom Alexander became acquainted was Mr. George Fulton, who, in addition to his duties as pedagogue for the community, also stood at the head of a Sunday school, — probably one of those which James A. Haldane and his co-laborer John Campbell had established during their famous visit to Greenock and other communities in the West of Scotland for that purpose, in the year 1797.[3] He was at pains to visit the Sunday school of Mr. Fulton,[4] — an act which must have won the favorable regards of that excellent person, for, when Alexander left the place for his sojourn in Glasgow, he was the bearer of a letter of introduction from Fulton to Mr. Greville Ewing.[5]

His arrival in Glasgow occurred on the afternoon of the 3rd of November 1808. Although he had been thoughtful enough to procure letters of introduction to several persons in the city,[6] it somehow befell that the

---

[1] *Ibid.,* vol. 1. p. 73.

[2] *Ibid.,* vol. 1. p. 69.

[3] *Ibid.,* vol. 1. p. 159.

[4] *Ibid.,* vol. 1. p. 108.

[5] *Ibid.,* vol. 1. p. 114.

[6] *Ibid.,* vol. 1. pp. 114-115.

letter to Mr. Ewing was the first which he was minded to present.[1] It secured him a night's lodging, and perhaps a large amount of well-deserved sympathy.

The next morning, having been informed that he was of the Seceder persuasion, Mr. Ewing gave him a note to the Rev. John Mitchel,[2] who, it is believed, was one of the two ministers of that order in Glasgow, Mr. Moutre being the other.[3] Mr. Mitchel was attentive enough to render him some degree of assistance in finding lodgings, perhaps in the house of one of his Seceder parishioners.[4]

But by some means Alexander seems to have already acquired a kind of distaste for the Seceders. The lodging which Mr. Mitchel had procured for the family was speedily concluded to be incommodious, and must needs be replaced by another of Mr. Ewing's selection, which was likely in the home of one of the members of his own church.[5] This may appear to be a trivial circumstance; but when we are reminded what an important effect the influence of Ewing produced upon the fortunes of the Campbell family, no transaction that fell out between them can wisely be overlooked. From this time Mr. Ewing was the chief counselor of the household, and his praises were on the tongue of every member of it.[6]

He was always ready to employ his good offices in their service. Through his courtesy Alexander was carried about and introduced to each of the professors of the university.[7] It was likewise, perhaps, by his assistance, that Alexander was enabled to make up those classes in the rudimentary branches which he taught in private for the purpose of improving the narrow finances of the family,[8] and by means of which it must have been rendered nearly impossible that he should make any solid progress in his own studies; a serious misfortune in view of the fact, that, by reason of the sad necessities of the situation, his early education had been left incomplete. At every point the toils of the excellent and plausible Ewing encircled the ingenuous and inexperienced boy. He was

---

[1] *Ibid.,* vol. 1. p. 128.

[2] *Ibid.,* vol. 1. p. 128.

[3] *Memoirs of Elder Thomas Campbell,* by Alexander Campbell, of Bethany, Va., Cincinnati 1861, p. 117.

[4] *Memoirs of Alexander Campbell,* vol. 1. p. 128.

[5] *Ibid.,* vol. 1. p. 130.

[6] *Ibid.,* vol. 1. pp. 148-149.

[7] *Ibid.,* vol. 1. p. 130.

[8] *Ibid.,* vol. 1. p. 139.

frequently invited to the house of Ewing in order to take dinner or tea;[1] before the winter was past, the disciple of Glas found himself on a decidedly intimate footing with the son of the Irish Seceder pastor.[2] Alexander had obtained a great impression of the learning and piety of his new friend,[3] and was soon as pliable under Ewing's manipulations as clay in the hands of the potter. Professor Richardson truly says, that his "stay at Glasgow was destined to work an entire change in the views and feelings of Alexander in respect to the existing denominations, and to disengage his sympathies entirely from the Seceder denomination, and every other form of Presbyterianism."[4] He is likewise correct in the admission that "the change seems to have been occasioned chiefly through his intimacy with Greville Ewing." Moreover, Ewing was esteemed "a very fine lecturer, and very popular both as a man and as a preacher, as was also Mr. Wardlaw, who frequently officiated." With Mr. Moutre, the pastor of the Seceder Church where his mother and the family attended worship, Alexander would naturally have small sympathy; and before the close of the winter his private notebooks exhibited various evidences of his impatience.[5]

It is not necessary to set down in further detail the features of this old and vulgar story, which has been enacted a thousand times before and since in many parts of the earth. It will be sufficient to call attention to the conclusion of it as recorded by the biographer of Mr. Campbell. Professor Richardson relates, that Alexander

> *became gradually more and more favorable to the principles of Congregationalism entertained by Mr. Ewing, which secured an entire emancipation from the control of domineering Synods and General Assemblies, and which seemed to him much more accordant with primitive usage. At the same time, he did not feel himself at liberty rashly to abandon the cherished religious sentiments of his youth, and the Seceder Church to which his father and the family belonged, and in which he thought it his duty to be a regular communicant.*
>
> *He was in this unsettled state of mind as the semi-annual communion season of the Seceders approached, and his doubts in regard to the character of such religious establishments occa-*

---

[1] *Ibid.,* vol. 1. p. 149.
[2] *Ibid.,* vol. 1. pp. 148-149.
[3] *Ibid.,* vol. 1. p. 187.
[4] *Ibid.,* vol. 1. p. 148.
[5] *Ibid.,* vol. 1. p. 187.

sioned him no little anxiety of mind concerning the proper course for him to pursue. His conscientious misgivings as to the propriety of sanctioning any longer, by participation, a religious system which he disapproved; and, on the other hand, his sincere desire to comply with all his religious obligations, — created a serious conflict in his mind, from which he found it impossible to escape. At the time of preparation, however, he concluded that he would be in the way of his duty, at least, and that he would go to the elders and get a metallic token, which everyone who wished to communicate had to obtain, and that he would use it or not, afterward, as was sometimes done. The elders asked for his credentials as a member of the Secession Church; and he informed them that his membership was in the Church in Ireland, and that he had no letter. They replied that in that case it would be necessary for him to appear before the Session and to be examined. He accordingly appeared before them, and, being examined, received the token. The hour at which the Lord's Supper was to take place found him still undecided; and, as there were about eight hundred communicants, and some eight or nine tables to be served in succession, he concluded to wait until the last table, in hopes of being able to overcome his scruples. Failing in this, however, and unable any longer to recognize the Seceder Church as the Church of Christ, he threw his token upon the plate handed round, and, when the elements were passed along the table, declined to partake with the rest.

It was at this moment that the struggle in his mind was completed; and the ring of the token falling upon the plate, announced the instant at which he renounced Presbyterianism forever, — the leaden voucher becoming thus a token, not of communion, but of separation.[1]

In brief words, the conquest of Greville Ewing and of his particular type of Sandemanianism was then first firmly established. Though he had entered Scotland comparatively innocent of these vagaries, Alexander turned away from the country at the end of three hundred days,[2] in a state of more or less abject slavery to them. With this view his own statement, made some years later in the pages of the paper which he edited in Virginia, is in agreement, where in speaking of the confirmed

---

[1] Richardson, *Memoirs of Alexander Campbell*, vol. 1. pp. 189-190.
[2] *Ibid.*, vol. 1. p. 194

disgust he felt against the "popular schemes" he adds, "which I confess I principally imbibed when a student at the University of Glasgow."[1]

Let the fact be likewise considered, that Alexander entered Glasgow on the 3rd of November, 1808, which left a period of not quite seven full months since the time when James A. Haldane had given such dire offense to Ewing and Wardlaw and the men of that faction, by submitting to the rite of immersion without waiting for their initiative. The circles in which he was received were by consequence very full of opposition to the course of the Haldanes in drawing near to the immersed wing of the Sandemanian fraternity. It is likely that Mr. Ewing and the church over which he presided had already taken the remarkable step by which they "refused to have visible communion with those who adhered to the Haldanes."[2] Alexander was, therefore, in no situation to hear the Haldane side of the controversy, and in no state of mind to do the Haldanes justice in case he had been permitted to hear it.

Accordingly it is perfectly natural that he should be inclined to favor the cause of the Sandemanians of the aspersion observance; and there is no good reason why Professor Richardson should find it somewhat singular, that during his residence in Glasgow none of the questions connected with infant-baptism and immersion engaged Mr. Campbell's attention in the least.[3] Ewing and his co-adjutor Wardlaw were both of them at the moment vehemently exercising themselves in opposition to immersion and to the baptism of adults only.[4] Alexander could have heard scarcely anything else than arguments in favor of infant-baptism and aspersion, at such times as he was admitted to a place at their tables. These disquisitions would naturally fall in with his previous convictions regarding those topics. He had not yet enjoyed an occasion to become intimately acquainted with the immersion wing of the Sandemanian body.

---

[1] *Christian Baptist*, edit. 6, p. 72
[2] *Memoirs of Alexander Campbell,* vol. 1. p. 181.
[3] *Ibid.,* vol. 1. pp. 186-187
[4] *Ibid.,* vol. 1. p. 187.

CHAPTER VII:
MR. CAMPBELL'S EARLIEST SUCCESS AS A PROPAGANDIST

Professor Richardson has, unhappily, left in a state of incompleteness that portion of his volumes which relates to the perversion to Sandemanian views of Thomas Campbell, the father of Alexander. It is very natural that he should be inclined to do as much honor as possible to the father of his hero; but in accomplishing this purpose he is suspected to have been, in some degree, unfaithful to the facts of history.

His readers must present their acknowledgments to the excellent author for the care he has often exhibited in permitting his characters to address the public in their own persons. Alexander Campbell seems to have been one of that kind of men who rarely ever lose a letter, whether the same were received or sent by him. Much of his early epistolary correspondence was strictly copied down in notebooks that he kept for the purpose of preserving documents that were of any sort of interest. A liberal share of the letters which passed between himself and his father, Thomas Campbell, have been reproduced in the pages of the biographer; but, singularly enough, not one of those is published which belongs to the time of Alexander's sojourn in Glasgow. This defect is to be regretted, since, if it were supplied, some light might fall from that source on the course of Thomas Campbell's proceedings during the same season in Pennsylvania.

In the narrative of Professor Richardson it is represented that Thomas Campbell had reached a position substantially like that to which Greville Ewing had brought his son, by means of his own private reflections and experiences, without any reference to communications that he might have received from Alexander while the latter was detained in Glasgow;[1] but this conclusion is, for several reasons, inadmissible. Everything, for example, that is reported of Thomas Campbell, whether in the volume which contains his own Memoirs,[2] or in the biography which Professor Richardson has supplied of his son Alexander, goes to show that he was a timid, inefficient person. There are no certain proofs that he was capable of independent thought or action, either at this or any other period of his life. The facts and instances which might serve to

---

[1] *Memoirs*, vol. 1. p. 220.

[2] *Memoirs of Elder Thomas Campbell*, by Alexander Campbell of Bethany, Va., Cincinnati, 1861

establish the propriety of this judgment regarding him are too numerous and circumstantial to be repeated here, but it would not be difficult to supply them on demand.

Moreover, it is not to be supposed that Thomas Campbell, in Pennsylvania, was kept in ignorance of the experiences of his family in Glasgow, nor of the kindness of Greville Ewing towards them, especially as every member of the household was glad to acknowledge the extent of their obligations to him.[1] The heart of the good and weak man would naturally be moved with gratitude towards the distant benefactor, and there would be no just bounds to his admiration for the greatness and power and condescension of the noble Sandemanian. Comparisons would easily be drawn between the kindness and attentions of Mr. Ewing, and the relative coldness and neglect of the Seceder minister, Mr. Moutre; and there would be no very careful reflections upon the circumstance that the distant bearing of his ministerial colleague might be due to the passion which his own loved ones had conceived for a disagreeable rival.

Again, it is entirely possible that Alexander was not slow to communicate the points of that intimate knowledge of Mr. Ewing's previous religious history which he had been enabled to acquire in the progress of his exceptionally friendly intercourse with him.[2] By means of this kind, Thomas Campbell, who, perhaps, was already in subjection to the imperious will of his son, would be placed in possession of several items of news that were highly acceptable to a husband and father in his own unfortunate situation.

By degrees, as Alexander found himself "gradually becoming more and more favorable to the principles of Congregationalism entertained by Mr. Ewing,"[3] various considerations in support of these would be included in his epistolary communications with his absent parent. These suggestions would each of them fall upon a mind and heart which had been prepared to receive them with cordiality. The father, in his rather exceptional weakness of character, would perceive that himself also sympathized with Alexander's distaste for the people among whom he was brought up, and with whom his fortunes had been the reverse of flourishing.

Under circumstances of this kind, it is not a matter of surprise, — it is only what might be reasonably anticipated, — that Thomas Campbell

---

[1] *Memoirs of Alexander Campbell*, vol. 1. p. 149.

[2] *Ibid.,* vol. 1. p. 149.

[3] *Ibid.,* vol. 1. p. 189.

should become involved in a controversy with the Seceders of the vicinity where he kept his residence. In the spring of the year 1809, while his family were still in Glasgow, a libel was laid against him in the Presbytery of Chartiers, "containing various formal and specified charges, the chief of which were, that he had failed to inculcate strict adherence to the Church standard and usages, and had even expressed his disapproval of some things in said standard, and of the uses made of them."[1] The case was appealed to the Associate Synod of North America, which convened in the fall of the year 1809. From the letter of protest that was addressed by Mr. Campbell at the time to this body,[2] it may be gathered that the objections urged against him related to the usual Sandemanian scruples concerning the impropriety of any human standards of belief, and to his advocacy of the customary Sandemanian position that the Scriptures are the only admissible standard, to the exclusion of all kinds of creeds and confessions of faith. Here was the earliest, if not the most brilliant, conquest which Alexander was enabled to make on behalf of Sandemanianism.

It is possible that the troubles which arose in the Presbytery of Chartiers were duly reported to the family, who were then abiding in Glasgow. Tidings of these occurrences may have reached their ears before the communion season already mentioned, at which Alexander was successful in making up his mind no longer to recognize the Seceder Church as the Church of Christ.[3] Although his case was pending before the Synod, Mr. Campbell did not leave off proclaiming the Sandemanian notions which had just met with decided opposition in the Presbytery. The churches of his Seceder brethren, it would appear, were promptly closed against his access; but he found accommodation for the people who were disposed to give heed to him, in the private houses of various persons who might be inclined to show him that favor.[4] In this labor of making propaganda for his new principles, he received special support from certain members of the Sandemanian Church in Rich Hill, Ireland, who had emigrated to America but a fortnight after he himself had come over.[5] Regarding one of these, who was the precentor of the Church, Professor Richardson truly says, "This James Foster was destined to take no unimportant part in Thomas Campbell's future religious move-

---

[1] *Ibid.,* vol. 1. p. 225.
[2] *Memoirs of Thomas Campbell,* by Alexander Campbell, pp. 12-15.
[3] *Ibid.,* vol. 1. p. 190.
[4] *Ibid.,* vol. 1. p. 231.
[5] *Ibid.,* vol. 1. pp. 81-83.

ments."[1] In fact, he was the faithful and efficient ally of Alexander in the efforts he made to draw his father away from his former allegiance to Presbyterian doctrines and polity.

Before the summer of 1809 was half closed, Thomas Campbell was engaged in meditating a scheme by which it might be in his power to put his new-found notions into practice. He proposed to his followers the propriety of holding a meeting for the purpose of imparting greater definiteness to the movement in which they were embarked. Perhaps it was some time during the month of May or June that one such was appointed at the house of Abraham Altars, one of his more subservient adherents.[2]

When that meeting had been duly convened and addressed, Mr. Campbell proposed, as a basis for all further action, the motto: "Where the Scriptures speak, we speak; where they are silent, we are silent." Here was, beyond dispute, an excellent ideal; but, in point of fact, it could hardly ever amount to anything more than an ideal. Neither Thomas Campbell, nor Alexander, nor any of their supporters has ever possessed wit enough to give effect to it by making out just where the Scriptures do speak. Great abuses once prevailed among them in that regard, which Alexander attempted to regulate by composing and publishing a fourth-rate treatise on the subject of Biblical Interpretation. Nothing was clearer than that the Campbells were hopeless failures in the department of exegesis, as most of their people have been; at any rate, they could lay no sort of claim to infallibility. Consequently it was impossible for them to apply their watchword to any advantage. What is the profit of professing to speak where the Scriptures speak, without more power than these gentlemen had to determine where the Scriptures speak or where they are silent?

However, the above motto was a neat and popular expression of the fundamental principle of Mr. Greville Ewing.[3] It is likewise nothing more than is professed in fact, if not in form, by every sect of religious worshippers in Christendom. Mr. Ewing and Mr. Haldane had both adhered to this motto with all the skill and devotion they could command, but with the sad result of perceiving, that, instead of the excellent Christian union which they so ardently desired, they were daily drifting farther apart. Ewing even felt himself constrained to deny any visible fellowship with the sometime friend and associate to whom he was un-

---

[1] *Ibid.,* vol. 1. p. 82.
[2] *Ibid.,* vol. 1. p. 231.
[3] *Facts and Documents*, pp. 124, 130.

der the deepest obligations for kindness bestowed. Nevertheless, he had not lost any portion of his faith in this watchword, believing that there was virtue in it to charm every discord that might arise in the Christian world. It is likely, that, in the mouth of Thomas Campbell, it signified nothing more important than, "Where Mr. Ewing speaks, we speak; and where he is silent, we are silent."

Whether the father or the son should be awarded the credit of imparting this taking expression to the leading principle of Ewing, is an inquiry that may not be easily determined. It is not unlikely that the first meeting and its incidents were duly and minutely reported to Alexander beyond the seas; he may have had knowledge of the whole business before he set sail for America on the 2nd of August 1809. The chief result of this preliminary meeting was not enacted until the 17th of August, when Alexander was already on the high seas. On that date was formed "The Christian Association of Washington," which appears to have been modeled in several respects after the pattern of the Haldanean "Society for Propagating the Gospel at Home," of which Thomas Campbell was a member during his residence in Ireland.

The first act of this Association was to issue a "Declaration and Address," the proofs of which were just coming from the press when Alexander arrived with the family at Washington, Penn., on the 28th of October 1809.[1] This document embraced a number of considerations in elucidation and advocacy of the principle that the Scriptures are in themselves a sufficient guide without the aid of any confession of faith or other kind of standard. It confined itself to somewhat narrow limits and general statements, its author not venturing to step beyond the boundaries which had been set for him in Scotland, through the example of Mr. Ewing, and possibly through the dictation of Alexander.

In the autumn of the year 1809, his letter of protest against the censure of the Presbytery of Chartiers was brought to the attention of the Associate Synod of North America, and along with it a copy of the "Declaration and Address" which in the interval had been published.[2] The Synod were kindly disposed towards him, and, reversing the action of the Presbytery, directed that he should be released from censure. At this point the narrative of Professor Richardson is confused and indefinite, but it suffices to indicate that the Presbytery were not content with the ruling of the Synod;[3] and at their next session, perhaps in the spring

---

[1] *Memoirs of Alexander Campbell,* vol. 1. p. 246.

[2] *Ibid.,* vol. 1. p. 228.

[3] *Ibid.,* vol. 1. p. 229.

of 1810, instead of dismissing the censure they renewed it, and referred the case back to the Synod. Thomas Campbell, conscious perhaps that his course was reprehensible, and for the moment unwilling to be debarred from religious communion, submitted to receive this second censure. However, instead of quitting his schismatical practices as the Presbytery now had a right to expect he would do, he persevered in them. Justly offended by his conduct, which they perhaps interpreted as a breach of faith, the Presbytery placed his movements under strict surveillance, with a view to their own protection, and in order to establish by undeniable proofs the correctness of their judgment against him when the Synod should again bring forward the case for review and decision. In this latter respect they were so far successful that the defendant himself must have become aware that it would be useless to continue the litigation. Accordingly, before the Synod met to consider the questions involved, Mr. Campbell found it prudent to hand in a formal renunciation of its authority, in which he declared that he should henceforth hold himself "utterly unaffected by its decisions."[1] These occurrences are supposed to belong to the autumn of the year 1810.

About the same time that he was engaged in declaring his independence of the Seceders, Thomas Campbell is found presenting an overture to the regular Presbyterians of the Synod of Pittsburg, praying for the reception of the "Christian Association of Washington" into their communion. That body heard him with respect while he unfolded the beauties of Mr. Ewing's principle, and then coolly dismissed him.[2] After this rebuff it was soon decided by the Campbells to organize a church of their own, a task which was accomplished at the regular semi-annual meeting of the Association, on the 2nd of May, 1811.[3] This church was organized as nearly as might be after the fashion of the one over which Greville Ewing presided in Glasgow.[4] It had weekly communion;[5] it maintained the biblical propriety of the independent form of church government;[6] it favored lay preaching in the same way Ewing did;[7] it did not adopt the notion of a plurality of elders, which Ewing also now rejected; and was content with choosing Thomas Campbell as elder, alt-

---

[1] *Ibid.,* vol. 1. p. 230.

[2] *Ibid.,* vol. 1. pp. 327-328.

[3] *Ibid.,* vol. 1. pp. 367-368

[4] *Ibid.,* vol. 1. p. 349.

[5] *Ibid.,* vol. 1. p. 373.

[6] *Ibid.,* vol. 1. pp. 345-346, and 349

[7] *Ibid.,* vol. 1. p. 346.

hough Alexander was licensed to preach.[1] Like Mr. Ewing, both the Campbells were still in favor of infant-baptism.

Nevertheless, out of regard for James Foster, the precentor of the Sandemanian Church in Rich Hill, who had refused even in Ireland to have his children baptized,[2] they were prevented from taking as definite grounds on that subject as their Scottish master was in the custom of assuming. Thomas Campbell, it would appear, strove hard to keep in the steps of Ewing in this quarter; but it was, perhaps, impossible for him to manage Foster. The Sandemanian precentor was highly scrupulous, and labored much to bring his friend over to his own way of thinking.[3] Under these circumstances there was no other resource than to make infant-baptism a matter of forbearance.[4] Considering the altered circumstances, this was keeping quite well in the track that had been marked out for them. "Mutual exhortation" also cut no figure at this moment in the Brush Run Church; Mr. Ewing, it will be remembered, had become disgusted with that item of "the ancient order of things" before Alexander's arrival in Glasgow, and was even charged by the Haldanes with turning against it.[5] Alexander was always unfavorable to it,[6] and opposed his influence when it was later introduced at Brush Run. Alexander must have frequently heard of the theological classes which Ewing was entrusted to teach during the first two years of his residence in Glasgow. The suggestion was not lost upon him. As early as he could after his arrival in Pennsylvania, steps were taken to organize a similar class. Its first, and, so far as reported, its only students, were James Foster and Abraham Altars.[7]

There was one single point, however, in which he had not yet learned to speak with Ewing. Whether that failure is due to the multitude of cares which must have beset him as the head of the family in Glasgow, robbing him of most of the leisure which otherwise he might have devoted to his studies; or whether he had a keener appreciation of matters relating to the "ancient order" than of such as related to the "ancient gospel;" or whether, in the third instance, he experienced a difficulty in the prospect of surrendering the view which he had always held concerning the nature

---

[1] *Ibid.,* vol. 1. p. 367.

[2] *Ibid.,* vol. 1. p. 82.

[3] *Ibid.,* vol. 1. p. 240.

[4] *Ibid.,* vol. 1. pp. 325 and 345.

[5] *Facts and Documents,* p. 126ff.

[6] *Memoirs of Alexander Campbell,* vol. 2. p. 128.

[7] *Ibid.,* vol. 1. pp. 277-279.

of saving faith, — must remain, for the present, a theme of conjecture. But, whatever should be the right explanation of the phenomenon, Alexander rejected, for a while, the conceit of Ewing and the Sandemanians, that faith is nothing other than mere belief, which is produced by testimony alone, without reference to the regenerating grace of God. On the 7th of April 1811, about twenty months after he had left behind him the advantages of the personal tutelage of his master, he is still found holding fast to the orthodox Seceder convictions regarding this subject.[1]

But the period was near at hand when he should accede to the notion of his master touching this point also, and, at the same time, go beyond him in other respects. The 7th of April 1811, is the latest date on which, according to the representations of his biographer, he was willing to affirm that faith "is of the operation of God, and an effect of almighty power and *regenerating grace.*"

The Brush Run Church which Alexander had succeeded in organizing out of the material that composed the "Christian Association of Washington," including his own, embraced the names of twenty-eight persons.[2] These were the first-fruits of his labors on behalf of the Sandemanian cause. He was untiring in his exertions, both in the neighborhood of his residence and elsewhere. On the 16th of May, 1811, he undertook his first missionary journey, which carried him into the State of Ohio, and gave him a store of experience, but a very slight measure of success.[3] In August he again went forth, and was employed most of the time until the close of the year; but the people were nowhere inclined to favor the innovations which he had borrowed from Scotland.[4]

---

[1] *Ibid.,* vol. 1. p. 376.
[2] *Ibid.,* vol. 1. p. 373.
[3] *Ibid.,* vol. 1. pp. 370-371
[4] *Ibid.,* vol. 1. p. 379.

CHAPTER VIII:
MR. CAMPBELL'S PERVERSION TO SANDEMANIANISM (Second Stage)

Already in boyhood, during his residence in Ireland, Alexander had become aware of the existence and the tenets of the Sandemanians of the immersion observance. His biographer is careful to note the fact that before the family departed from Rich Hill, he had "been much pleased with the works of Archibald McLean, especially his work on 'The Commission,' of which he was wont ever after to speak in the highest terms."[1] This incident is of importance to the student of his life and changes.

The Brush Run Church does not appear to have enjoyed a great degree of harmony of conviction in its efforts to "unite on the Bible." On the third day after its organization, a question was raised that must have given the members an amount of solicitude. When the Lord's Supper was celebrated for "the first time on Sunday, the 4th of May 1811, it was remarked that three of the members — Joseph Bryant, Margaret Fullerton, and Abraham Altars —refrained from the elements. Upon inquiry made for the reasons which might influence them to pursue this course, it was discovered that neither of them had ever been baptized after any of the various modes in which that ordinance is administered among Christian communities.[2]

The difficulty would have been of easy adjustment if these parties had been willing to accept baptism by effusion. In that instance there would have been no kind of obstacle in the way of Thomas Campbell's speaking where Mr. Ewing spoke. But they were unhappily decided in their conviction that the "ancient order of things" provided for baptism by immersion. Joseph Bryant would likewise appear to have taken the lead in making the demand for this form of the ordinance,[3] and he was a person whom it was exceedingly desirable to conciliate. Besides the fact that he had rendered most efficient service in erecting the house of worship at Brush Run,[4] it may also be mentioned that he had been an attentive member of "The Christian Association," and perhaps already was recognized as an eligible match for Miss Dorothea Campbell, to

---

[1] *Ibid.,* vol. 1. p. 71.

[2] *Ibid.,* vol. 1. pp. 371-372

[3] *Ibid.,* vol. 1. p. 372.

[4] *Ibid.,* vol. 1. p. 322.

whom he was united in marriage about twenty months later, on the 13th of January 1813.[1] It was, therefore, very trying to resist Mr. Bryant's conscientious scruples and his earnest solicitations.

On the other hand, Thomas Campbell was loath to depart from the platform of Greville Ewing. A discussion of two months' duration was carried on, at the end of which Bryant was successful. Mr. Campbell immersed him and his two friends on the 4th of July 1811.[2] But this concession to the wishes of a few did not mend the condition of affairs; it only whetted the appetite for other changes. James Foster, the Sandemanian precentor, who witnessed it, was not edified by the manner in which the ceremony was performed. Instead of entering the water along with the subjects, the administrator stood on the root of a tree at the side of the pool, bending down their heads until they had been covered by the water. Furthermore, in order to signify the position which he had now brought himself to occupy, Foster expressed the opinion that it was incongruous for one who had not been baptized in his own person, to administer the rite to other people.[3] Manifestly it was becoming daily more impracticable for the Campbells to walk in Ewing's way. They must either leave it, or submit to witness the Church which they had established at Brush Run go to pieces. An earnest discussion had been some time going forward on the subject of immersion,[4] and it was not a great while before "many of those connected with Thomas Campbell had advanced beyond him." They were restrained from carrying out their convictions, and submitting to this form of the rite, by nothing else than "the respect which they felt was due to his position."[5]

Alexander seems now to have perceived that speedy action must be had, else their cause was lost. He therefore resolved to take the step which it was becoming evident the larger portion of the Church demanded at the hands of himself and his father. Accordingly he made preparations to procure his own immersion.[6] When he went to communicate his intention to his father, an ally was found in the house in the person of his sister Dorothea.[7] Naturally concerned to avoid an explosion in the Church, by means of which she might be required to decide

---

[1] *Ibid.,* vol. 1. p. 458.

[2] *Ibid.,* vol. 1. p. 372.

[3] *Ibid.,* vol. 1. p. 373.

[4] *Ibid.,* vol. 1. p. 393.

[5] *Ibid.,* vol. 1. pp. 399-400.

[6] *Ibid.,* vol. 1. p. 395.

[7] *Ibid.,* vol. 1. p. 395.

between the affection she bore her parents, and her affection for the man to whom she was, perhaps, already betrothed, she had become, like Mr. Bryant, a decided advocate of immersion. If Bryant, and the majority of the little community at Brush Run, could have been induced to tolerate aspersion, it is probable that the Campbells would never have found it convenient to leave the side of the sprinkling Sandemanians.

But affairs had taken a direction which it was not in their power to control, and they were compelled to follow the current. Alexander's previous acquaintance with the treatise of Archibald McLean on "The Commission of Christ" must have now done him a service, giving him a rudder by which to steer his course. The father, then as always pliant before the stronger will of his son, was not disposed to offer any serious objections, and at the last moment decided to be immersed himself.[1] The event occurred on the 12th of June 1812; the rite being performed by a Baptist minister of the Redstone Association, named Matthias Luce. Four days afterwards, thirteen other members of the Church were immersed by Thomas Campbell. The remainder, who would not accede to the new change, went their way, leaving behind them a Church of twenty members who were united in approbation[2] of the course that had been pursued, and whose clamors perhaps had made it necessary. James Foster was one of the thirteen.[3]

A circumstance of personal concern to Alexander also had a certain share in the business of directing his attention to these issues. On the 13th of March 1812, his first child was born. The question of infant-baptism, therefore, became to him a topic of special interest. Doubtless with reference to the scruples of James Foster, he had formerly urged that this point should be treated as a matter of forbearance.[4] That was the utmost limit to which he might safely advance if he desired to retain the sympathy and support of so important a personage. It does not appear that he had even ventured as far as that since the 5th of June 1811, possibly abstaining through fear of provoking an undesirable conflict. If now he had dared to baptize his own child, after its birth in March 1812, he must have done so with the conviction that the act would cost him the affections and the countenance of most of the communicants at Brush Run. At any rate, he could not make up his mind to provoke the Church in that way; and, contrary to the position of Greville

---

[1] *Ibid.,* vol. 1. p. 376.
[2] [Approval]
[3] *Ibid.,* vol. 1. p. 403.
[4] *Ibid.,* vol. 1. p. 392.

Ewing, his child was compelled to dispense with baptism.

The winter of 1811-12 was in other directions an eventful one for the Brush Run Church. Foreseeing that he would be constrained by the force of circumstances to take final leave of Mr. Ewing, Alexander began to take further lessons in the "ancient order." Before the first day of January 1812, he had become convinced of the propriety of maintaining a plurality of elders in every church;[1] and on that day he was ordained, possibly in order that the Church might be provided with a Presbytery after the Sandemanian model. On the occasion of Thomas Campbell's removal from the vicinity, in the year 1813, James Foster was ordained in his place, that the Presbytery might not be destroyed by his absence.[2] Plurality of elders had now, to all appearances, become the article of a standing or falling Church.

While yet a resident of Rich Hill, Alexander had been made personally acquainted with one John Walker, a learned and unfortunate gentleman whose literalism had rendered him one of the most fantastic of all the Sandemanians.[3] He was so far gone in the "ancient order" that he "sold his carriage and travelled on foot through Ireland, and also through England," proclaiming the virtues of an exact conformity to the minutest details of it.[4] During the season here under review, Alexander seems to have returned to his youthful admiration for this exceedingly queer head. He attentively perused his writings, and to a degree made him the man of his counsel.[5] It was from Walker, perhaps, that he obtained the singular notion about religious communion, which on the 26th of February 1812, caused him to question the propriety of family prayer wherever the family might be composed in part of unbelievers.[6] As has been already shown, numbers of the Scottish Sandemanians refused to maintain family prayer; but these generally referred their objections to a literalistic interpretation of the injunction which ordains that men shall enter into their closets alone, and there address the heavenly Father in secret. They likewise made much of the fact that there is no distinct biblical command enjoining in so many words the duty of praying in the family. The form in which Alexander's scruple was indicated, however, suggests rather the influence of Walker.

---

[1] *Ibid.,* vol. 1. p. 385.

[2] *Ibid.,* vol. 1. pp. 458-459.

[3] *Ibid.,* vol. 1. p. 61.

[4] *Ibid.,* vol. 1. p. 61.

[5] *Ibid.,* vol. 1. p. 466

[6] *Ibid.,* vol. 1. pp. 447-449; cf. p. 61

The admiration he felt for this impossible character was never abated. In his last years he condemned himself because he had not kept closer to Walker's rigid and exclusive principles.[1] As a specimen of that gentleman's extraordinary proceedings, it may not be amiss to mention a visit he made to Edinburgh, perhaps to confer with the Haldanes, who went very far in the direction of restoring "the ancient order." The usual Sandemanian custom prescribes the Lord's Supper on every Lord's Day. But Walker could find nobody in all the city who was good enough to enjoy this rite of religious communion, except the travelling companion who had made the journey with him, and a single student of medicine in the university. These three ate the elements alone.[2] Professor Richardson also records the fact that Walker's spiritual arrogance was cultivated to such an extreme "that it was a special point with him, strictly to prohibit the performance of any religious act without removing to a distance (if in the same room) from every person who refused to obey a precept that could be generally applied; insisting that true worship could be rendered only by those who receive and obey the same truths in common"[3]

The arrogance of the Scottish Sandemanians did not always carry them quite so far, but it was not unusual for principles of this kind to be applied in the public worship of their churches on the Lord's Day. A Sandemanian Church of the immersion observance had been established in the city of New York, in the autumn of the year 1810, under Elders Henry Errett and William Ovington, which was quite as fantastic an institution as one could reasonably desire. In the customary style of the party, they rejected all human creeds, rules, covenants, thinking the Scriptures perfect enough for direction in everything. Church edifices were no part of the "ancient order of things," neither were pulpits: they hired a hall, and claimed that it was not possible elsewhere to witness the sight of a church assembled together.[4] This body held four public services in the week, at neither of which were any but communicants admitted; at another public service appointed for Tuesday evening, they were willing to see the outside world, and to preach the gospel to them.[5] In the year 1818, they had so far mended their manners as to permit the "world" to attend on Sunday evenings, after the regular worship of the Church had been concluded, at which time the elders, and

---

[1] *Ibid.,* vol. 1. p. 454.

[2] *Facts and Documents*, p. 247.

[3] *Memoir of Alexander Campbell,* vol. 1. p. 61.

[4] Benedict, *History of the Baptists.* Boston 1813. Vol. 2. p. 409

[5] *Ibid.*

some others of the brethren approved by the Church, would be gracious enough to declare the gospel to them.[1]

By some means Alexander had become aware of these ridiculous proceedings of the immersed Sandemanians, and was immediately captivated. He resolved to copy them in that as well as in so many other singularities; and when, after his immersion, the Brush Run Church was re-organized on the basis of the "Scotch Baptists," no person "was recognized as duly prepared to partake in religious services, except those who had professed to put on Christ in baptism."[2]

The absurd tenor of his sentiments, and the sincerity of his conversion to these idle puerilities, may be illustrated by the fact that when he attended the session of the Redstone Association, in August 1812, he could not be induced to preach before the outside public, as other ministers were in the custom of doing. Every solicitation of that kind was declined. On the contrary, he was willing to discourse one evening in a private family to some dozen preachers and twice as many laymen.[3] This conduct would be inexplicable on any other supposition, except that Alexander's motto seems now to have suffered an alteration, by means of which it should read, "Where the Scotch Baptists speak, we speak;" and not many of these could be found who went to more wretched extremes.

Thomas Campbell, as usual, was the obedient echo of his son in the suggestions made by the latter in favor of this arrogant policy of exclusion.[4] If the father and son had but followed that policy continuously and consistently, it is not in the least probable that our country would have been burdened with the shame and evils of Mormonism, — which grew out of the Disciples' movement, — since their influence would have been so much circumscribed that their enterprise could have affected few persons besides themselves and their immediate dependents.

A portion of the winter of 1811-12 was also devoted to the task of acquiring the doctrine and the dialect of the Sandemanians in relation to faith. In a letter directed to Mr. Robert B. Semple in April 1826, Alexander informs him that he had "appropriated one winter season for examining this subject."[5] The facts, however, as they are set down by his biographer, show that this was not an entirely correct reminiscence; for,

---

[1] *Christian Baptist*, p. 389.
[2] *Memoir of Alexander Campbell*, vol. 1. p. 454.
[3] *Ibid.*, vol. 1. p. 440.
[4] *Ibid.*, vol. 1. pp. 449-454.
[5] *Christian Baptist*, p. 228.

in addition to his investigations regarding the nature of faith, it is clear, from what has been said above, that he also found time to investigate and accept the Sandemanian doctrine concerning the plurality of elders; to change his mind about the action of baptism and about the propriety of infant-baptism; to adopt the notions of the Sandemanians of the straightest sect in favor of excluding from the worship of the Church all persons who were not members of the Church; and to discuss the absurd proposition to discontinue family prayer in cases where all the members of the household might not be fortunate enough to relish the fantastic conceits of the party to which he was now inclined. He had long previously made the discovery upon which the average Sandemanian was likely to value himself, to the effect that Sunday is not the Jewish Sabbath day; but it was only during the winter in question, that the sentiments of himself and the community which he led became so much the topic of public remark as to excite the report that they "paid no respect to the Sabbath."[1]

Returning to the subject of faith, Alexander describes as follows the method in which he pursued his investigation:

> "*I assembled all the leading writers of that day on these subjects. I laid before me Robert Sandeman, Hervey, Marshall, Bellamy, Glas, Cudworth, and others of minor fame in this controversy. I not only read, but studied, and wrote off in miniature, their respective views. I had Paul and Peter, James and John, on the same table. I took nothing upon trust. I did not care for the authority, reputation, or standing of one of the systems, a grain of sand. I never weighed the consequences of embracing any one of the systems as affecting my standing or reputation in the world. Truth (not who says so) was my sole object. I found much entertainment in the investigation; and I will not blush, nor do I fear to say, that, in this controversy, Sandeman was like a giant among dwarfs. He was like Samson with the posts of Gaza on his shoulders.*"[2]

It would have been nearly impossible for a person of his present connections and situation, especially one who was so much lacking in respect to independence of mind and theological capacity and culture, to have reached a different conclusion. Here, as at so many other points, Alexander was the unquestioning slave of his masters.

---

[1] *Ibid.,* vol. 1. pp. 432-435.
[2] *Christian Baptist*, p. 228.

In case the representations made by Professor Richardson are complete, the revolution which took place in Alexander's mind, by which he became a subject of Sandeman in the matter of faith, began in the month of October 1811,[1] and was completed in the month of March 1812.[2] In connection with it he carried forward a correspondence with his father, perhaps chiefly for the purpose of showing him deference. The harmless old gentleman was incapable of rendering any considerable assistance in his enterprises, but it was in his power to offer a deal of resistance in case he were not duly coddled and conciliated. As on every other occasion, Thomas Campbell played the role of a convenient echo. It is surprising to witness the readiness with which he could repeat at first blush such Sandemanian watchwords as "the bare belief of the naked truth," and affirm, against the convictions of a lifetime, that this "involuntary, un-avoidable faith " was sufficient to procure salvation.[3]

In requesting baptism at the hands of Matthias Luce, Alexander, in due subjection to the authority of Archibald McLean as laid down in his work styled "The Commission of Christ Illustrated," says he had stipulated "that it should be performed *into the name* of the Father, etc., and not *in the name*, as was then and now is usual among the regular Baptists."[4] Moreover, it was not his object, in seeking immersion, to unite with the Baptists of America. On the contrary, he declares, "I had no idea of uniting with the Baptists."[5] Not many months had passed by, however, before that purpose entered his mind; and in order to accomplish it he was willing, in the month of August 1813, to violate one of the leading Sandemanian tenets, and to contradict the teachings of the famous "Declaration and Address," by composing for the purpose a sort of confession of his faith, which, if it could now be procured, would possibly supply an amount of interesting reading.[6]

But he was never at that or any other moment, either by sympathy or by conviction, a Baptist. In a private letter under date of Dec. 28, 1815, more than two years after his Church had been received into the fraternity of the Redstone Baptist Association, he describes his situation in the following terms: "I am now an Independent" (or Sandemanian) "in Church government; ... of that faith and view of the gospel exhibited in

---

[1] *Memoir of Alexander Campbell*, vol. 1. p. 413.

[2] *Ibid.*, vol. 1. p. 422.

[3] *Ibid.*, vol. 1. p. 419.

[4] *Memoirs of Thomas Campbell*, p. 114.

[5] *Memoir of Alexander Campbell*, vol. 1. p. 439.

[6] *Ibid.*, vol. 1. p. 440.

John Walker's seven letters to Alexander Knox; and a Baptist in so far as respects baptism."[1]

During the period between the year 1812 and 1820, Alexander relapsed into a condition of mere vegetation. In the year 1816, he was able to excite a small controversy by a discourse on "the law" before the Redstone Association, where, in keeping with his Sandemanian principles, he thought the preaching of the gospel was sufficient to produce the "bare belief of the bare truth," and therefore maintained that it was unnecessary and reprehensible to persuade men by the terrors of the Lord. He also became to a degree interested in the missionary cause,[2] which the Redstone Association was then prosecuting with some kind of vigor.[3]

The year 1820, however, was full of events that supplied him fresh incitement, and opened for him a career. The month of April brought him a newspaper discussion on the question regarding the Sabbath,[4] in which he embraced an opportunity of setting forth and maintaining the customary Sandemanian distinctions with much length and logomachy.[5] The month of June brought him an oral discussion about the action and subjects of baptism, with the Rev. Mr. Walker of the Seceder Church. These occurrences served to arouse him from his long-continued lethargy, as well as to call the attention of circles to his abilities as a rhetorician, which had not previously been aware of his existence.

---

[1] *Ibid.,* vol. 1. p. 466
[2] *Christian Baptist*, p. 17 and p. 72
[3] Benedict, *History of the Baptists*, New York 1856, p. 615.
[4] *Memoir of Alexander Campbell*, vol. 1. p. 522.
[5] [Dispute about words]

CHAPTER IX:
BAPTISM FOR THE REMISSION OF SINS

The most important impulse that the year 1820 had in store for Mr. Campbell was conveyed to him in a doctrinal pamphlet that was published and sent forth by the "Scotch Baptist" Church of New York City. This body was, perhaps, pleased to regard itself as, in a certain sort, the leader of sentiment among the churches of that persuasion in this country. The pamphlet referred to was largely devoted to a treatment of the design of baptism. It was forwarded, we may suppose, to all the Sandemanian churches of the immersion observance in America, if not also to those in the British Islands as well. One of these existed at the moment in Pittsburg, under the pastoral supervision of Mr. Walter Scott, one of the principal co-laborers of the Campbells. A copy was conveyed to him. The work also fell into the hands of Alexander and his father.[1] They all perused it with more or less of avidity;[2] it was the subject of a number of eager conferences between the trio.[3] Alexander had it on his mind at the debate with Walker and ventured to employ the position which it maintained in one of his addresses against the practice of infant-baptism, asserting that "baptism is connected with the promise of the remission of sin and the gift of the Holy Spirit."[4]

Here was the beginning of a new departure. The document of the New York Church contains the same view regarding the design of baptism to which the Campbells later gave in their adhesion;[5] it was also published by Scott in one of the numbers of "The Evangelist," a monthly periodical which he edited respectively in Cincinnati and Cambridge, O. The same texts which the sect of Disciples (or Campbellites) are in the habit of setting forward are produced in this pamphlet, and handled much in the same way, in order to support the conclusion that baptism was designed for the remission of sins.

But Alexander was disposed to approach this business in a gingerly fashion. It was manifest that the sentiments advanced by the men of New York were nothing else than a development of the views expressed by Archibald McLean, the father of the "Scotch Baptists," in his famous

---

[1] *Life of Elder Walter Scott*, by William Baxter, Cincinnati 1874, p. 47.
[2] [Eagerness]
[3] Richardson, vol. 2. p. 83.
[4] *Ibid.,* vol. 2. p. 20. [See Acts 2:38]
[5] *Life of Scott*, by Baxter, pp. 47-53

work entitled "The Commission of Christ," which had been for many years in the hands of the Campbells. At that place this author declares, "To be baptized *the remission, or washing-away, of sins,* plainly imports, that in baptism the remission of sins is represented as *really conferred* upon the believer. The gospel promises in general, 'That, through Christ's name, whosoever believeth in him shall receive remission of sins.' Baptism applies this promise, and represents its *actual accomplishment* to an individual believer, assuring him that all his past sins are now as really washed away in baptism by the blood of Christ, as his body is washed in water." [1] He also says, "As to the *necessity* of baptism to salvation, it is no stronger expressed in these passages [John 3:5, and Tit. 3:5] than in some others concerning which there is no dispute, such as, 'He that believeth and is baptized shall be saved' [Mark 16:16]; 'The like figure whereunto baptism doth also now save us,' etc. [1 Pet. 3:21]; 'Be baptized, and wash away thy sins' [Acts 22:16]." [2]

But from the manner in which McLean, in this work, guards some of his utterances, it might be in the power of an opponent to affirm that it was not entirely warrantable to represent that author as a thorough-paced advocate of the theory of baptismal remission. His New York followers, on the other hand, had fully, and without much hesitation, taken their stand upon this dogma. Alexander, however, is considered to have felt some misgiving as to whether these gentlemen were of canonical authority. It is not, perhaps, entirely accidental, therefore, that, in his published version of the debate with Mr. Walker, he appears on both sides of the issue touching the design of baptism. [3] Nevertheless, the question was not of small concern to him. The topic of the New York pamphlet was often the theme of remark. [4] When the *"Christian Baptist"* was sent forth in the year 1823, it was among the first matters that were put forward for treatment. In the second number of the periodical, under date of Sept. 1, 1823, an article that bears the marks of careful preparation is published, in which the writer confidently takes his stand on the side of the New Yorkers, and pleads the propriety of the sentiments which were enunciated in their pamphlet of the year 1820. Thomas Campbell, who was not responsible, and whose opinions could easily be disclaimed in case any

---

[1] See McLean's *Commission,* edit. 1, p. 133.

[2] *Ibid.,* pp. 131-132, note. A Disciple firm of publishers in Cincinnati, O., have republished this work from the third Edinburgh edition. In the year 1871 there had been five editions of the American reprint.

[3] Compare Richardson vol. 2. p. 20, with vol. 2. pp. 36-37.

[4] Richardson, vol. 2. p. 83.

strong objections were heard against them, was put forward in this way to feel the public pulse.[1]

In the month of October 1823, Alexander was engaged in a public debate with the Rev. Mr. McCalla, a Presbyterian divine, at Washington in Mason County, Kentucky, in which the action and the subjects of baptism were again treated. Here he likewise found courage enough to endorse the New York authorities in his own proper person, by setting forth the position and the arguments which, they had employed in their publication.[2] But he was still so much disposed to hesitate regarding their canonicity, that his scruples at a later date more than once took him over to the other side of the issue.[3]

In October 1824, a second advance was made towards the principles which the New York Sandemanians had laid down; and Thomas Campbell was in this instance likewise employed to perform the delicate task, Alexander being still in a state of incertitude regarding the question whether it would be prudent and popular for him to espouse their cause. The article which his father was now employed to write was of twice the length of that which he had previously produced, and in some respects more decided.[4] In December 1824, the father again engages to enlighten the "professing world" upon the significance and importance of what the New York theologians had laid so heavily upon his own mind.[5] Various other expedients were devised to keep the point before the public. In the month of May 1826, a writer who appears under the *nom de plume* of "Independent Baptist," who is suspected to be no other than Alexander, asserts in round terms "that the baptismal water washes away sin, and is the only Divinely appointed pledge that the blood of Christ has cleansed the conscience of the obedient disciple."[6] That his mind was strongly engaged in that direction, may also be perceived from occasional references to the topic which are elsewhere scattered up and down in the pages of his periodical. Among these, attention may be directed to the more or less covert allusions on p. 94, p. 118, and p. 351, respectively.

In October 1827, he contrives to throw off a portion of his constitutional timidity, and to employ in his own person language that, with considerable definiteness, signifies that he had now made up his mind to

---

[1] *Christian Baptist*, pp. 11-13.
[2] Richardson, vol. 2. pp.80-83.
[3] *Christian Baptist*, pp. 58, 67, 70, 64.
[4] *Christian Baptist*, pp. 99-101
[5] *Christian Baptist*, p. 115.
[6] *Christian Baptist*, p. 236

become an avowed convert to the New York theory. He says, "Elder John Secrest told me, at the meeting of the Mahoning Association, Ohio, on the 27th ult., that he had immersed three hundred persons within the last three months. I asked him, '*Into what* did he immerse them?' He replied, he 'immersed them into the faith of Christ for the remission of their sins.' Many of them were the descendants of Quakers, and those who had formerly waited for the baptism of the Holy Spirit in the Quaker sense of those words. But brother Secrest had succeeded in convincing them that the *one baptism* was not that of Pentecost, nor that repeated in Caesarea, but an immersion into the faith of Jesus for the remission of their sins. . . . Thus while my friend Common Sense, and his two Baptist doctors, are speculating on what regeneration is, brother Secrest has by the proclamation of repentance towards God, and faith in the Lord Jesus Christ, and immersion for the remission of sins, been the means of re-generating three hundred in three months, in the proper import of the term."[1]

These statements have the appearance of being uttered by a person who had finally made up his mind to assume a definite position and to maintain it against all who might come forward to oppose him. Moreo-ver, the seed that, since the year 1820, he had been sowing with so much care and covert art, had already taken root in some quarters. In more than one section of the country persons who chanced to be under his influence were proclaiming the conceit of the New York Church. During the year 1826, Jeremiah Vardeman had been advocating it in Kentucky, and professed to entertain a degree of satisfaction in administering the ceremony of baptism that was superior to anything he had known before he was rightly instructed in the New York theory.[2] B.F. Hall was also on the same ground, with the same message, in the same year of grace.[3] Adamson Bentley and Jacob Osborne were declaring it to the people of Ohio in 1827, as well as John Secrest already mentioned above.[4] It was indeed high time for Alexander, if he desired to remain at the head of the movement, to declare in public his adhesion to the notion of baptismal remission.

But a number of trials were still to meet him before he should finally gain his consent to formally announce his acceptance of what seemed long since to have become his favorite tenet. Walter Scott, who in other

---

[1] *Christian Baptist*, p. 381

[2] Richardson, vol. 2. pp. 287-288.

[3] *Ibid.,* vol. 2. pp. 388-389

[4] *Ibid.,* vol. 2. pp. 207-208

years had been his co-laborer in Pittsburg, was appointed, at its session in September 1827, as the missionary of the Mahoning Association in Ohio. This arrangement had been effected under the oversight and largely through the influence of Alexander, and he hoped that many advantages might accrue from it in the way of perverting the Baptists of that body to Sandemanian opinions and customs.[1]

Notwithstanding the circumstances that Elder Scott had been often admitted to conferences that were held touching the New York notion,[2] and though, as Campbell declares, he had been definitely advised by Scott to introduce that opinion into the debate with McCalla in October 1823, yet this person, if one may judge from his writings in the *"Christian Baptist,"* prior to November 1827, had never contrived to get any practical hold or understanding of that tenet. Nay, when he heard it promulgated by Jacob Osborne in the early autumn of 1827, it is said to have struck him with surprise.[3] Not long afterwards, however, he was, by some agency of which no distinct account has been given, made sensible of the meaning and importance of the new departure which Alexander had been pushing ever since the reception of the circular about baptismal remission, in the year 1820; and he took hold of the idea with his customary enthusiasm and precipitation. The first discourse that he delivered in favor of it was not rewarded by any visible results.[4] It served the purpose, however, of rendering him broad awake to the excellency of an opinion which a number of his brethren in the vicinity where he was laboring had been some length of time proclaiming. The only apparent obstacle in the way of his action in thus going forward lay in the fact that he was occupying an official relation to the Mahoning Baptist Association, and it was wholly uncertain how that body would be disposed to regard this flagrant departure from the *principles of the Baptist community.* Alexander was justly uneasy regarding the issue, especially since, in case the churches which had employed Scott should repudiate him, the most of the blame would attach to himself, who had perhaps suggested this expedient, and selected his long-time associate and disciple for the position.

Notwithstanding the manifest perils of the situation for his principal, Scott, in the enthusiasm of a new convert, was resolved to press forward. On the 18th of November 1827, he appointed a meeting at New Lisbon,

---

[1] *Ibid.,* vol. 2. pp. 173, 174; cf. p. 206.
[2] *Ibid.,* vol. 2. p. 83.
[3] *Ibid.,* vol. 2. p. 208.
[4] *Ibid.,* vol. 2. p. 209.

Ohio, in which he announced that he would fully discuss "the ancient gospel."[1] Here at his first discourse he secured his earliest convert; and this may be set down as in some sort the natal day of the modern Disciple movement. Before the series of meetings at New Lisbon were concluded, Scott had succeeded in persuading seventeen persons to be immersed for the remission of sins.

This conduct on his part rendered it necessary that he should make a speedy visit to the leader of the movement at his residence in Virginia.[2] The two friends must have discussed the hazards to which the precipitancy of Scott had exposed their cause in Ohio, and the probabilities that he had effected the destruction of Alexander's hope to pervert the entire Association from the doctrines which they had hitherto maintained. The situation was indeed critical, and the slightest mishap would have brought upon them extreme disaster. Scott's energies were therefore excited to their fullest tension; it was necessary to accomplish the work of perversion as far as possible before the date appointed for the next session of the Mahoning Association, in order that objections which might be confidently anticipated should be silenced, or that the party of opponents might be defied. In this enterprise he was successful to a high degree; and from the 18th of November 1827, the notion of baptism for the remission of sins was *officially* recognized as a part of the faith of the Disciples.

In January 1828, Alexander got courage enough to lend a helping hand by commencing a series of articles in the "Christian Baptist," on the "ancient gospel," where he comes out boldly on behalf of the opinion which hitherto he was in doubt whether he should publicly and irrevocably avow. By a very adroit contrivance he is skillful enough in the first of these to represent John Secrest, a Kentucky preacher of the Stoneite or Christian party, as proclaiming this opinion with distinguished success on the Western Reserve. "Elder John Secrest," he reports, "told me on the 23rd of November, in my own house, that, since the Mahoning Association last met, he had immersed with his own hands one hundred and ninety, thus lacking only ten of five hundred in about five months — for it is not more than five months since he began to proclaim the gospel and Christian immersion in its primitive simplicity and import."[3]

This second allusion to the labors of Secrest would be, at that moment, a desirable diversion in favor of Scott, by assuring the people of

---

[1] *Ibid*, vol. 2. p. 210 and p. 212.
[2] Hayden, *History of the Disciples in the Western Reserve*, p. 93.
[3] *Christian Baptist*, edit. 6, p. 402.

the region where they were both employed that the latter was not alone in the innovation that he was practicing. But at a later time, when Scott manifested a disposition to claim the most of the credit for the prosperity and success of the Disciples' enterprise, the above extract was the occasion of an amount of ill feeling. Scott appears to have conceived the idea that Campbell was jealous of him, and had inserted the statement that has been cited with the purpose to deprive him of his just honors.

CHAPTER X:
OTHER ITEMS

The founder of the Disciples was highly reticent regarding the nature and extent of his obligations to the Sandemanians, whether of the aspersion or of the immersion observance. The occasions were comparatively rare when he could be induced to reveal his counsels in that direction. At the head of the *"Christian Baptist"* he had placed as a motto the passage, "Style no man on earth your father, for He alone is your Father who is in heaven, and all ye are brethren;" and it was considered important, that, in accordance with this injunction, little should be reported concerning the Sandemanians, who were his own masters on earth. It was likewise an element of strength in that class of the community whom he had access to, that he should make a large parade of his intellectual independence, and sometimes of his "erudition,"[1] a quality with which he was also but moderately provided.

William Jones, who, after the death of Archibald McLean, became the leader of the "Scotch Baptists," or Sandemanians of the immersion observance, embraces the opportunity to disburden his mind regarding this clear instance of ingratitude, which was provided by a letter he addressed to Mr. Campbell on the 16th of March 1835.[2] From the representations there set forth, this kind of "childish vanity" must have been the common failing of a number of those churches which, in Ireland and America, had descended from the "Scotch Baptists." John Walker, the fellow of Trinity College, Dublin, for whom, even down to his latest days, Mr. Campbell felt an extravagant admiration, is sorely chastised for his crimes of omission at this point. Mr. Jones professes to be able to prove that Walker owed his earliest impulse in favor of Sandemanianism to the writings of Archibald McLean, and pities "those individuals who, through the pride and envy of their hearts, have scorned to acknowledge their obligations to the servants of God whose labors have been so useful to them."[3]

In America he is particularly severe upon the conduct of the New York Church, for their neglect to feel any gratitude towards those Churches in the Fatherland to whom they owed much thanks. Speaking of the circular which had been sent forth by that organization, in the year

---

[1] McCalla, *Debate on Baptism*, Buffalo 1824, p. 124.

[2] *Millennial Harbinger*, 1835, pp. 298-300.

[3] *Ibid.,* p. 299.

1818, to many of the prominent "Scotch Baptist" Churches in England and America, regarding the "ancient order of things," and afterwards published under the title of "The First Part of an Epistolary Correspondence between the Churches in America and Europe," Mr. Jones complains, that, "though it is well known that those individuals had gone out from this country, and carried their principles with them, there is not the smallest reference, in all their narratives, to the source whence they derived them."[1] Nor does he quite spare the Disciples, reminding Mr. Campbell that he would not deny that his own churches took their origin from the "Scotch Baptists."[2]

In reply to these just complaints, Alexander allows his personal obligations, but is content to express these in terms of such shadowy generality as in effect almost to deny them. At the close of the letter in which these concessions are made, he adds, "But now, Brother Jones, after all these acknowledgments for myself and my brethren, I have no hesitation in saying that there will be found views of the Christian institution *wholly new*, as far as the works of all the schools to which I have alluded are concerned. This I say not from vanity, nor from pretensions to originality; but from a conviction, before God, that it is due to all the citizens of Christ's kingdom, in Europe and America, to state that the cause we plead is at least something in advance of even the Scotch, or English, or American Baptists, as I have no doubt will appear to yourself from a careful examination of the books forwarded you."[3]

It must be conceded that he has embraced some items in his creed which may not be found in the works of his masters, the "Scotch Baptists." These were immediately insisted upon by Mr. Jones with so much emphasis as to defeat the hopes which at one time Alexander would seem to have entertained to the effect that it might be in his power to swallow up the "Scotch Baptists," and celebrate another triumph of that Christian union which he professed to believe would in the end destroy all "sects and sectism" by comprehending every one of the various Churches of the Christian world in his own Church. This would have been a splendid ambition if it had not been supremely ridiculous.

The most important particular in which he departed from the theology of the "Scotch Baptist" writers consists in the fact that he surrendered the Calvinism in which he had been educated, in favor of Arminian sentiments. In the present state of research, it is not possible to

---

[1] *Ibid.,* p. 298

[2] *Ibid.,* p. 300.

[3] *Ibid.,* pp. 306-307.

suggest the precise time and circumstances in which Alexander accomplished this change. His biographer is entirely at fault here, and leaves the reader wholly without information. Indeed, both himself and his hero appear to have been fresh enough to believe that they were not really Arminians as long as they omitted to designate themselves by that title, no matter how firmly and consistently they might profess and support Arminian principles. This policy, which after the fashion of the ostrich leads them to imagine that they are sufficiently concealed by covering their head in the sand, is one of the most amusing foibles of the Disciples.

However, it would appear that as late as the year 1811, Alexander had not yet turned away from his Calvinistic convictions; since in his notes on the writings of John Walker, made at that season, he has set down, apparently with approval, the substance of one of his author's chapters against Arminianism.[1] He was likely still in favor of Calvinistic views as late as the 28th of December 1815, on which date he informed his uncle Archibald, in a letter addressed to him in Ireland, that he was "of that faith and view of the gospel exhibited in John Walker's seven letters to Alexander Knox."[2]

There have been few more absurd hyper-Calvinists than was John Walker, and it would be difficult to embrace his "faith and view of the gospel" without in some degree partaking of that sentiment. But in the absence of more definite information regarding the portion of Mr. Campbell's life that lies between 1811 and 1820, it would be in vain to speculate about the date and circumstances of his perversion to Arminian opinions. We must content ourselves with the simple fact that when he began to set forth a printed record of his position, in the *"Christian Baptist,"* he was already a confirmed opponent of the system of the Calvinists. Thomas Campbell was permitted to retain his Calvinism, but only as a sort of philosophy, or other attenuated appendage. In this sublimated capacity it would do no great amount of harm, while it might serve to remind them of the source whence they had sprung, and upon occasion to furnish a bond of sympathy with the "Scotch Baptists," in case it were deemed prudent at any time to attempt the project of effecting a union with them.

It must be allowed that Mr. Campbell's adhesion to Arminian views suited much better with his theory of baptismal remission, than the

---

[1] Richardson, vol. 1. p. 446.
[2] *Ibid.,* vol. 1. p. 466

Calvinism in which he had been reared and trained. To discard the system of Calvin for the behoof of the New York theory, and to embrace Arminianism in its stead, would at least indicate that he had an eye for symmetry.

A very considerable result of this abandonment of Calvinism appears in the fact that Mr. Campbell was thereby enabled to deny the doctrine which he had preached in his early time, that spiritual influences of some sort must co-operate with the word before the sinner will exercise faith. According to the scheme of the "ancient gospel" which Walter Scott elaborated, the operations of the Holy Spirit must be confined entirely to those who are already in a saved estate. His much-boasted *ordo salutis* was: (1) Faith, (2) Repentance, (3) Immersion, (4) Remission of sins, and (5) The Holy Spirit. To the Third Person of the Trinity was conceded unchecked access to the hearts of believers; but it was not allowed him to influence the hearts of unbelievers, and it was sometimes even attempted to show that the act of faith was such an easy matter that there was no need of his assistance in order that it might be effected. Nevertheless, the leaders of the movement had a deal of trouble to explain the circumstance, that, since faith is wholly the result of testimony, some of those who attended their own ministry should accept the testimony they were in the custom of imparting, while others of equal or superior capacity for sifting and weighing testimony would turn unaffected away from it.[1]

This same arbitrary method of dictating to the Holy Spirit what might be the sphere and limits of his operations may be found in the writings that the Congregational minister, Mr. W. Cudworth, sent forth in his controversy against Robert Sandeman, which have already been mentioned on a previous page.[2] Cudworth also advanced, in the same works, the singular hypothesis that the word of Scripture is the Spirit; a fancy that was approved and elaborated in the well-known Dialogue between Timothy and Austin, which Mr. Campbell sent forth in the pages of the "Harbinger."[3]

In the winter of 1811-12, which Mr. Campbell appropriated to the examination of these issues, the work of Cudworth was one of the books that he studied. Writing to his father on the 28th of March, 1812, Alexander says, "I have read about one-half of Cudworth this week. Will give you my sentiments respecting his performance in my next."[4] Un-

---

[1] Richardson, vol. 1. p. 427, and vol. 2. pp. 150-163. [

[2] William Jones of England, in the *Millennial Harbinger*, 1835, p. 443.

[3] *Ibid.*

[4] Richardson, vol 1. p. 425.

happily Professor Richardson has failed to insert the letter in which his cogitations about the production of Cudworth are recorded. If that were supplied, it is possible that a degree of assistance might accrue to the labors of students in this department. As the writings of Cudworth cannot be consulted at the present moment, it is not possible to form a conclusion with any degree of detail as to how far the positions assumed by Mr. Campbell may correspond to the opinions which that singular author has enunciated. It is just to state, however, that Mr. Campbell assures his English critic that he reprobates the notion of Cudworth.[1] It is equally just to add that this same notion is distinctly advocated in the Dialogue between Timothy and Austin.

Mr. Jones likewise informs us that those persons in England who took up with the opinion of Cudworth "have, in process of time, verged into Socinianism or Deism, among whom were some of the elders of our (Scotch Baptist) Churches." According to this account, therefore, the immersed Sandemanians of the mother country were affected by these extraordinary conceits touching the Holy Spirit, as well as their brethren under the lead of Mr. Campbell in America. And it is further no secret at all that Mr. Campbell and a portion of his adherents were much suspected of a leaning towards the tenets of Socinianism or Arianism. This suspicion was aroused at an early period, — even before the Disciples had entered upon any official church relations with the Unitarian followers of Barton W. Stone in Kentucky, — as may be seen in the pages of the "*Christian Baptist*," pp. 50 and 216. For a number of years he was at great pains to clear himself and his people of imputations of this nature that were laid against them. After the comprehension of the Stoneite party in Kentucky, these suspicions became more numerous than ever; and it was a tedious task to meet the objections that were excited by that action.

It is hardly necessary to ransack the literature of the Sandemanians of Europe for traces of the distinction that was so much approved and employed by Mr. Campbell, between faith and opinion, and is the chief prop of the Plea for Christian Union. Nothing could be more easy than to fall upon this expedient without the aid of a special counselor. The appearance of arrogance which induces him to assert that the confessions of faith, set forth by various Christian churches, are merely confessions of opinion,[2] is not an unusual display in the ranks of the smaller sects. In

---

[1] *Millennial Harbinger*, 1835, p. 463.
[2] *Christian Baptist*, p. 216.

general, the opinion of Mr. Campbell, touching the meaning of a given passage of Scripture, was too likely to be regarded as a point of faith, while the equally careful and honest conclusions of others who, to say the least, were not less competent than himself, were somewhat haughtily denounced as unworthy of that high distinction. In the debate that occurred between himself and the Rev. N.L. Rice, at Lexington, Ky. (Nov. 15 to Dec. 2, 1843), he was sorely pressed to declare the point where faith begins and opinion ends,[1] but was not able to bring forward any satisfactory reply.

Nevertheless, the distinction proved to be practically serviceable in enabling his people to comprehend within their communion a number of persons believing in Unitarian and Universalist tenets, who were willing to promise that they would hold this item of their faith as a mere opinion. It was not long, however, until he was constrained to deplore an unfortunate condition of affairs, and to complain that "all sorts of doctrines, by almost all sorts of men," were proclaimed among his adherents.

The different sects and systems which we have been considering are extreme, and in several respects fantastic, developments of the principles of Protestantism, and especially of that principle which asserts the necessity of returning to the Bible as the standard of faith and action. The literalism which is an abuse of Protestantism was pretty well displayed in each of them, and in several instances it became absurd and injurious.

In conclusion, it is believed that the statement with which the present treatise was begun has been shown to be true. The Disciples of Christ are the direct descendants of the Sandemanians; it is possible to point out in the literature of Sandemanianism the source whence Mr. Campbell derived almost every one of his religious opinions. If he ever had an original idea, he took pains to avoid giving expression to it in such of his writings as have been submitted to the inspection of the public.

---

[1] Debate with Rice, p. 813.

ORIGIN

OF THE
DISCIPLES OF CHRIST

A REVIEW OF PROF. W H. WHITSITT'S VOLUME ENTITLED
"ORIGIN OF THE DISCIPLES OF CHRIST."

A Contribution to the Clearer Understanding of the Origin and Principles
of the Religious Reformation Inaugurated by Thomas and Alexander
Campbell, Near the Beginning of the Present Century.

By GEORGE W. LONGAN,
MINISTER OF THE CHURCH OF CHRIST.

To WHICH IS ADDED AN APPENDIX
CONTAINING EXTRACTS FROM
Reviews of Prof. Whitsitt's Book by Baptist Writers

WITH AN INTRODUCTION BY J. H. GARRISON,
EDITOR CHRISTIAN-EVANGELIST.

1889

INTRODUCTION

It has been said that a grain of wheat or barley, found in the sarcophagus of an Egyptian mummy, where it had lain dormant many long centuries, when placed in the earth, germinated, grew, and multiplied itself many fold. Whether this incident be true or not it is certain that many seeds are covered with a flinty case or envelop which protects them in a dormant state for years, until they are surrounded by favorable conditions, when they awaken to life and develop all their germinal potentiality. The history of the world's progress shows that this is pre-eminently true of those seed-thoughts which, from age to age, have been sown in the minds of men, and whose ultimate harvests have furnished bread for the world's hunger. Truth is the most indestructible of all potencies. The men who speak it may indeed pay the penalty of their lives for its utterance, but the truth they utter lives on to guide the course of history.

> *"Truth forever on the scaffold;*
> *Wrong forever on the throne;*
> *Yet that scaffold sways the future,*
> *For behind the dim unknown*
> *Standeth God within the shadow,*
> *Keeping watch above his own."*

"It was during the fiercest dogmatic controversies and the horrors of the Thirty Years' War," says Dr. Philip Schaff, in his *Ecclesiastical History* (Vol. VI., page 650), "that a prophetic voice whispered to future generations the watchword of Christian peace-makers, which was unheeded in a century of intolerance, and forgotten in a century of indifference, but resounds with increased force in a century of revival and reunion: 'IN ESSENTIALS UNITY, IN NON-ESSENTIALS LIBERTY, IN ALL THINGS CHARITY.'"

This famous saying, sometimes referred to St. Augustine, and oftener to Richard Baxter, who quotes it, is traced by Dr. Schaff to Rupertus Meldenius, an otherwise unknown divine and author of a remarkable tract, in which the sentence occurs. This tract, it is believed, appeared in the year 1627 or 1628. Fifty years later, however, Baxter quotes it, from another author in the preface to his work on "The True and only way of Concord of all the Christian Churches." And now, in the latter part of the 19th century, two hundred years later, I am quoting this same great truth in the Introduction to another work, which, I have no doubt, offers a far better solution of "the true and only way of concord of all the Christian churches!"

Here, then, is an admirable illustration of the indestructible vitality of an important truth, which not only persists in living through centuries of opposition and neglect, but which manifests increased power over each succeeding generation. How few there were to recognize in this statement the germ of a great religious reformation, when it was first formulated and uttered by Meldenius! In Baxter's day it attracted more attention as offering relief from the interminable strifes and divisions with which all pious, truth-loving souls were weary. But it was not until more than a century later that it gained practical recognition in an organized movement having for its end the unity and peace of the church.

Indeed, it is quite certain that neither Meldenius nor Baxter perceived all that was involved in this memorable motto. What they did see, evidently, was an utter lack of discrimination, in the popular mind, between the things which are vital and those which are incidental, and the consequent effort to enforce uniformity at the expense of unity. As a remedy for this state of things they proposed the foregoing statement which had in it the seed of a reformation yet to be. But the seed must wait for genial soil and favorable surroundings. If either of the men named, or any of the theologians of that period who accepted this motto, had been asked to state more specifically what were the "things essential," and what the "things indifferent," their answer, doubtless, would have borne the marks and the limitations of the religious thought of their times. It was for another age to develop, more clearly than was possible at that time, the right application of this principle to the religious problems upon which Christendom had divided into hostile camps.

In the early part of the present century, Thomas Campbell, looking at the same evils which Meldenius, Baxter, and others had seen and deplored, uttered a not less remarkable saying in the memorable words which he made the battle cry of reform: "Where the Scriptures speak, we speak, and where the Scriptures are silent, we are silent." The clear import of this striking motto was. What is enjoined upon men by divine authority we shall insist on being observed; and where the word of God has left men free, we shall not bind them. The phrase, "things essential," had now been interpreted to mean, *the things required by the Scriptures*, and the "things indifferent" were those where the *silence* of the Scriptures left men free to follow their best judgment. In both these mottoes there is a clear recognition of divine authority, and an equally distinct rejection of human authority in matters of religious faith and practice. In each of them there is a solemn emphasis of loyalty to God, on the one hand, and of freedom from the tyranny of opinion, on the other. But "where the Scriptures speak" is a decided advance, in the direction of clearness and definiteness, beyond the "things essential."

In the progress of the Reformation as urged by the Campbells and their co-laborers, another distinction of great value came into vogue. The "things essential" of this 17th century motto, and the things enjoined by the Scriptures, were called *matters of faith,* while inferences on matters where the Scriptures are "silent," — the "things indifferent" — were called *matters of opinion.* This distinction between faith and opinion — the one resting on divine authority, the other on men's fallible judgment — served to clear away a good deal of fog from the religious atmosphere, and to enable men to go forward in the work of reform with a firmer step. It was now seen that a great many things which properly belonged to the category of inferential knowledge, and might be classified as such, representing the results of Biblical investigation, could never be classified as belonging to the *things of faith,* or have any legitimate place in a creed or confession of faith. It was the clear perception of this distinction that led our reformatory fathers to reject, *as bonds of union and communion,* all human creeds and confessions of faith. It was not that these creeds contained errors, though doubtless they did, being the results of fallible human thought, but that they contained matter which, whether true or false, had no business in a *creed* or confession of *faith,* to serve as a basis of fellowship among Christians. If true, they belong to the category of inferential *knowledge,* not of faith. If they suggested wise methods of organization, work or worship, they belonged to the "things indifferent," and not to "things essential."

In the historical evolution of this reformatory principle, there was yet another step taken, which was essential to the application of this venerable motto to the religious questions of the age, and necessary to bring the reformers clearly on to New Testament ground. It was soon perceived in the light of New Testament teaching, that the faith which the gospel requires — the truly evangelical faith — was faith in Jesus of Nazareth, as the Christ, the Son of the Living God. It was not faith in dogmas, propositions, or ordinances, but in a *Savior,* that constitutes saving faith. To believe in *him,* and to obey his commandments *because* we believe in him — these, now, it was seen, were the "essential things," in which there must be "unity." Other matters, not contravening these, were the "things indifferent," concerning which there must be "liberty." How significant, now, the saying of Paul, "There is one faith! "Many *opinions* there may be, but there is only one *faith,* having for its object the one Lord. Here, at last, was perspicuity itself. The magnificent generalization, coined by Meldenius and adopted by Baxter, when illumined thus by the light of the New Testament, became an operative principle. Only men were now needed with the courage of their convictions, to test this principle in the practical work of reform. The men were not wanting. They did test it; and with what results the world knows.

The origin and development of a great religious movement, which, in less than three quarters of a century has gathered together in one body, from the world and from all the discordant sects of Christendom, more than three quarters of a million of adherents, who, without other bond of union or basis of fellowship than that possessed by the primitive church, maintain unity in things essential without restricting liberty in things indifferent, is a subject that might well engage the careful thought and the impartial treatment of the student of church history and of religious progress. The book of which this volume is a review seeks the origin of this movement in certain accidental or incidental ecclesiastical relations, or fortuitous contact of individuals by which strange and peculiar notions and practices were transmitted through the leaders of the movement and embodied in what is termed the current reformation. *This* volume, on the contrary, with a truer historic insight, sees in this religious movement the orderly development and timely embodiment of great fundamental truths, which, taking their source in the very nature and organic life of the Christian institution, have, after centuries of slight and neglect, found more or less perfect expression in the utterances of men who lived ahead of their time, until in the fullness of time, in a freer age and in a freer land, they have found opportunity for manifesting their divine potency. It is more than a reply to the warped opinions and far-fetched inferences of Prof. Whitsitt. It is a broad, scholarly, dignified discussion of the underlying *principles* of our movement, which, without following in detail the animadversions of the book it reviews, none the less effectually removes the foundation from beneath it. The author evidently feels that no mechanical theory about "offshoots" or imaginary similarities between our movement and some supposed heresy of former times can harm us, so long as it can be shown that we build on the same foundation on which the apostles built, and hold fast to those principles which have made Christianity the conquering power that it has been in the world.

That this volume will contribute to a clearer understanding of the fundamental law — the *raison d'etre* — of our movement on the part of all who read it thoughtfully, I cannot doubt. That it may, also, serve to hasten that unity for which our Lord prayed, I fain would hope and pray.

St. Louis, April 1, 1889.

J. H. Garrison.

CHAPTER I:
PRELIMINARY

There are Baptists and there are *Baptists*. That is to say, there are Baptists who are large-minded, Christian men; there are others that are narrow, illiberal, bigoted: genuine old time Pharisees, as it were, only dipped and newly named. Those of the one class are gratified to see differences disappearing, old animosities gradually dying out, and more fraternal relations growing up between themselves and other disciples of the Lord. The rest are, apparently, never quite so happy as when stirring up old strifes, fanning the fires of party hate, and making men imagine themselves enemies who ought, long ago, to have seen clearly that they are brethren in Christ. With those of the former class, it is our duty and pleasure to cultivate brotherly love and mutual respect; as for the other sort, it is sufficient if we sincerely pray that their eyes may be opened, and patiently bide the Lord's time for the answer to our prayers.

"The Origin of the Disciples?" That should be an interesting inquiry. Of course, the surface facts are common property. Disciples and Baptists are alike familiar with them. But there is a deeper question, one which the philosophers of a later generation are certain to deal with, and which it is to be hoped they will be better able to answer, than are the jaundice-eyed sectarians of the present time. This is a day when men are looking after *origins* with an interest which was never felt before. The birth of worlds, the beginning of life, the derivation of species, the differentiation of social structures and functions, in the ever-increasing complexity of civilized life, the evolutions of thought, the castaway blunders, the survival of tested hypotheses, which have marked the progress of human knowledge from the dawn of the historical period, to the present year of grace, — these are the questions concerning which the thinkers of our time consider it worthwhile to employ their highest powers. In such a period, the *origin* and development of a movement which clearly contains within it the "promise and potency" of most wonderful achievements for God and our fellow-men may well challenge the attention of honest inquirers after enduring reality. This search after *origins* is a most fascinating pursuit. There is nothing like it. And whether it relates to the processes by which the insignificant tadpole gets rid of its tail and gills, and acquires legs and lungs, a phenomenon occurring every year before our eyes, or that more ancient transformation, in which the land-lubber whale of the elder moons became — not exactly a fish, for that he is not — but monarch of the seas, for all the historical ages, it makes no difference at all. It is in any case a question of *origin*, and, as such, it has that nameless fascination, which you are not able to explain, but which, nevertheless, excites an interest that nothing else in the wide field of human investigation is able to arouse within you. The *origin* of the Disciples! That is the question now. Prof. Whitsitt has been rummaging the theological records of the eighteenth century, and has found, or *thinks* he has found, in those far away times, traces of an obscure sect, which presents homologous characteristics with those which he says distinguish the Disciples at present, or did distinguish them a generation or two ago, and, straightway, he springs to the conclusion that here is a clear case of genetic development. "The Disciples are an offshoot from the Sandemanians." This is their *origin.* This explains why they are here, and also how they came to be here!! Then the Sandemanians were adjudged great heretics by some people in their day, and therefore the Disciples of Christ must be heretics too. So the case seems fairly made out, and, doubtless, the achievement will be judged of sufficient importance to warrant the addition of other titular honors to those which our learned Professor displays in connection with his name on the title- page of his small, but somewhat pretentious book.

But really, now that we come to think of it, what does this matter of ancestral lineage amount to after all? Even if the case were confessedly clear that the Disciples came from the Sandemanians, would that fact make them either better or worse? The question of genetic descent is doubtless one of great philosophic interest, but what has it to do with the status of any man, or any community of men, now living? Should the Anglo-American of today concern himself greatly in regard to the proportion of Saxon, Angle, or Jute blood that courses in his veins? Is he either better or worse for any possible combination of these ancient elements? Or, considering the question from the ecclesiastical standpoint, are any of us better or worse because our ancestors, a few generations back, were Roman Catholics? Or, if in making their way out of spiritual Babylon, our forefathers have struggled along this or that dimly lighted pathway, what does it signify? A man's grandfather was, let us say, a Presbyterian, but he is, himself, a Baptist. His great grand-father was a Roman Catholic. The question of his descent, genetically, either by blood or ecclesiastic affiliation, is of no practical significance. The interest which attaches to such a question is purely scientific or philosophical. The important matter is not that of descent, but of *ascent.* Have the generations through which he counts his lineage been going up or down? Does he represent, in his own person, a lower or higher altitude?

This is the only question worth a groat, when we are dealing with the claims of a religious community. I may be greatly interested in tracing the interactions of the human mind with its social or ecclesiastical environment through many centuries, in noting how, and when, it has disengaged itself from this false speculation, or that rank superstition, and emerged into a clearer and better intellectual atmosphere; or perchance I may note periods of decadence, of reactionary tendencies, when the wheels of progress have been reversed, and the mind has gone backward, instead of forward to its divinely predestined goal. In point of fact I am greatly interested with such studies. But I hope to be always able to distinguish between the scientific interest of such an inquiry and that of the moral and spiritual significance of its final outcome. What we are today is everything; what our forefathers, in any sense, were a hundred or five hundred years ago, is nothing. How the race began, along what physiological or biological lines it may be compelled to trace its progress when science has uttered its final word, does not affect at all the question of man's rank and dignity at the present time. My thoughts about Christ, about the gospel of Christ, are neither sound or unsound on account of the traceable interactions of a thousand generations through which they have been shaping themselves into their present form. The Disciples of Christ are to be judged by their faith and life today, just as Baptists are, and not by any real or imaginary connection with generations dead and gone. And this I say without conceding any value whatever to Prof. Whitsitt's assumption of a genetic relationship between the Disciples and the Sandemanians of more than a hundred years ago. Even if his case were made out, it is still nothing; but it is not even made out.

Why a Baptist, of all the men in the world, should start this question of lineage is scarcely clear. There is no denominational appellative more indefinite than Baptist. Why, how many sorts of Baptists are there, anyway? Let us see. There are, or there have been, *Regular* Baptists, *Separate* Baptists, *Calvinistic* Baptists and *Armenian* Baptists; *Seventh Day* Baptists and *Six Principle* Baptists; Baptists that were for sending missionaries to the heathen, and Baptists that were opposed to sending missionaries to anybody. I need not further specify. Prof. Whitsitt knows them all. I make no comment. Only I remark, in passing, that, in view of these facts, I fail to see why a Baptist Professor should concern himself greatly about questions of ecclesiastic origin.

CHAPTER II:
A BRIEF INQUIRY INTO THE NATURE OF "OFFSHOOTS"

No great movement of any kind ever owed its origin to a single individual. When we speak of the beginning of the Reformation of the 16th century, we designate it the Lutheran Reformation on account of Luther's great prominence in its inception and early progress. But when we say "The Lutheran Reformation," if we are not lamentably ignorant of its history, we mean no more than the assignment of due precedence to the most distinguished among a great number of able and equally faithful men. And if we should imagine that there were no influences at work, no deeply felt dissatisfaction with the existing order of things, no strong intellectual and moral tendencies slowly shaping themselves for future effect, before Luther appeared on the scene, we would betray very gross ignorance of some of the most significant facts of history. The seeds of Protestant truth were already germinating in many hearts when the monk of Erfurt began his remarkable career as a reformer. The Catholic Stawpitz, who said to Luther, vainly seeking peace through the intercession of saints, and the holy virgin, "You would be a painted sinner, and have a painted Christ as a Savior," was already, though unconsciously, much more than half a Protestant. And how much, for good or ill, did Luther owe to Augustine, the greatest of the Latin fathers? It was Luther himself who said, "Next after the Holy Scriptures, no teacher in the church is to be compared with Augustine; take the entire body of the fathers together, there is not to be found in them half that we find in Augustine alone." We may differ from him in this estimate. The subtle but profound insight of the earlier Grecian school at Alexandria was clearly underrated by him. But the point I press is Luther's indebtedness to others, and the fact of pre-existing tendencies, which shaped his thought, and determined the mighty work of his life. The greatest men that have ever lived have been made what they were, in large part, at least, by the outward conditions — providential, let us devoutly say — which surrounded them in the youthful and plastic period of their careers. It was, I believe, the thoughtful and brilliant Frenchman, M. Taine, who said that the "Protestant movement" (I quote the meaning, not the precise words) "would have been impossible at the time, in any other country of Europe than Germany." *A great movement in the world's living thought must have an adequate preparation.* Next to Germany,

England was the best field for Protestant missionary effort. Wycliffe, "The Morning-star of the Reformation," and Tyndale, the translator and martyr, did not live and suffer in vain. M. Taine well say "that England was more than half Protestant when Henry VIII. found himself driven to separation from Rome." Not by any means the least interesting feature in Dr. Neander's great history of the church is the scholarly and painstaking minuteness with which he traces the evolution of ideas, disclosing thereby the hidden forces by which all important changes in the exterior course of things had been gradually wrought out. Uniformitarianism is the law of human history, no less than that of the planet on which we live. That there have been exceptional periods, periods of relatively great and rapid changes, is in no sense contrary to the general fact. He has been a very superficial student of mundane events who has not made this discovery, and learned to apply it discriminatingly in dealing with the history of particular periods, or tracing the inception and progress of great and enduring movements in the thought and lives of men.

If the 18th century was not marked by any great original movement in theology, it was still a period of very considerable intellectual activity along certain lines of doctrinal speculation. The ablest minds, while fairly content with general results of the earlier creative period of the Reformation, were sedulously striving to systematize and reduce to scholastic form the essential elements of the common Protestant outline; but each one, of course, in his own way, and from his own individual point of view. This led to many minute inquiries and hair-splitting distinctions, very much after the manner of the older scholastics, which we are apt in this more practical age to set aside as useless. Among these nice and sometimes puzzling distinctions, must be reckoned much that was said and written on the nature of faith, especially "saving faith," and precisely how this faith is related to justification, so that, although it must be conceded to be, in some sense, the act of the creature, yet the doctrine of grace is not impaired by making it the sole human ground of divine acceptance. In this special field, Glas and Sandeman, from our distant point of view, appear to have been adventurous pioneers, leading bravely out into what doubtless seemed to them to be the most promising paths of inquiry which the researches of the fathers of Protestantism had left open to their descendants. They were keen thinkers, if not profound, and their speculations, though often unfruitful as judged by the standard of our times, must be admitted to have been ingenious, and sometimes absolutely convincing. They did more than attract the attention of the best thinkers; they made a marked impression upon the thought of their age. But Sandemanianism, as the system came to be designated, was not limited to ingenious speculations concerning the nature of faith and justification, but embraced the more practical questions of the organization and order of the churches in the times of the apostles, and while yet under their personal instruction and authoritative guidance.

They saw that there had been no unbroken line of continuity in the outward succession of history. Comparing the organization and order of the churches of their own time with what they read plainly in the *New Testament*, they saw that a very great change had taken place. There were no state churches in the beginning. And this was not simply that the secular administrations of the period were unchristian, or anti-christian. They felt that neither Christ nor the apostles would have tolerated for a moment the idea of an Established Church. With Glas, this had been the original point of departure from the beaten path of his fathers. But the Bishops and clergy, the reverend ministers of all the received orthodoxies, were quite distinct in their order and official relations from the simple and unostentatious Bishops and Evangelists of the *New Testament*. They insisted, therefore, upon a reconstruction in harmony with the *New Testament Scriptures*. In this contention the day of judgment will undoubtedly vindicate their wisdom and faithfulness, even though some men may think they were misled by an overstrained "literalism" in the attempts which they made to realize their conception of the constitution of the original churches of Christ. Why should it be thought a vicious "literalism" to adhere closely to primitive precedents in the matter of organization and order, as well as in other things? Especially, one is tempted to ask, why should Baptists urge such a view as this? The Baptists, whose sole distinction almost relates to the ordinances? Are the ordinances everything, and the original order nothing? Why then do Baptists talk about their "faith and *order*"? Or is it so, that rigidness as to the subject and "mode" of Baptism must be maintained at all hazards, but that the office, and relations to the churches, of the divinely constituted Bishops, Deacons, and Evangelists is judged of no importance at all? If this be so, why is it so? On what ground is rigidness demanded in one case, and any desirable laxity admitted in the other? What is the exact limit, beyond which, "literalism" in following the apostles ceases to be a virtue? Or is this the explanation — viz: that Prof. Whitsitt *thinks* the Baptists are in line with the apostles on the ordinances, and *knows* that, on the questions of organization and worship, they are to some extent out of harmony with them? This I suppose to be the true reason in spite of the sneers at an undefined "literalism" by means of which he seeks to conceal the fact in the case.

But Glas and Sandeman finished their course without accomplishing anything which could be called epoch-making in its character. They lived and died Pedobaptists, and also rigid Calvinists. It is of the first importance that the reader should not forget these facts for a single moment. He should need nothing more to keep him from being misled in the matter now under discussion.

Prof. Whitsitt will find it impossible to make intelligent Disciples feel the least respect for his attempt to trace their origin to such an unlikely source. Nor will he be able to persuade well-informed outsiders that there is even honest plausibility in his partisan contention. What he may succeed in impressing upon certain portions of his Baptist constituency, is, indeed, another question, but one of no very great importance. Only those who have an "unction from the Holy One" are proof against the wiles of partisans, and the followers of Christ should be prepared to "endure contradiction" in the spirit of their divine Master.

After the Sandemanians, we are asked to find our ecclesiastical lineage in the Scottish Baptists — "so called." The order of progress is assumed to be; firstly, the Sandemanians; secondly, the Scotch Baptists; thirdly, "the Disciples of Christ, commonly called Campbellites." Indeed these Scottish Baptists are not really Baptists at all, but only "Sandemanians of the immersion observance." This is no doubt a very clever phrase, and we should take pleasure in giving its inventor due credit. Let us hope there is no one entitled to contest Mr. Whitsitt's claim to originality in this case. But then why not let us speak of the Baptists in this country as "Congregationalists of the immersion observance," while their New England congeners are styled "Congregationalists of the aspersion observance?" Such a mode of designation would be quite as plausible, certainly, and not a particle less worthy the respect of truth-loving men. The points of agreement between Baptists and Congregationalists are quite as numerous, while those of difference are as few, as in the case of the Sandemanians and Baptists of Scotland. Nor are the differences more important in the one case than in the other. With all fair-minded people, this statement will be accepted without a moment's hesitation. And, if the Scotch Baptists were only "Sandemanians of the immersion observance," then the American Baptists are no more than Congregationalists, who have been dipped by an administrator who had himself been duly dipped *by someone else!* How far the line of dipped administrators extends backward towards the apostles, neither Prof. Whitsitt nor any other Baptist could tell if his salvation depended upon it! There are some things that one finds it hard to treat with respectful consideration. And if any dear Baptist brother, who loves Christ and the truth more than he loves his party, should think I have written any words here in style too flippant for grave themes, let him remember that all such words are to be strictly limited to the author of this book and the bellicose class of Baptists to which he properly belongs. As regards the Scotch Baptists, they agreed in a general sense with the Sandemanians concerning the "nature of saving faith," and they followed the New Testament, as did also the Sandemanians, both in the matter of church organization and in observing the Lord's Supper, as part of the worship on the Lord's day. If this made them Sandemanians, then I insist that the Baptists of the United States are singly English Puritans modified by local influences, and the personal idiosyncrasies of their partisan leaders. If the Scotch Baptists were narrow literalists in some of their notions concerning the invariable order of worship on the Lord's day, their American cousins are quite as narrow, and scarcely less the slaves of "the letter" in restricting the Lord's Supper in their churches to those who belong to the Baptist "order," or hold membership in distinctively Baptist churches. The reproach of narrowness, or servile literalism, comes with poor grace from Baptists of the Graves and Bay school, to which the author of this book seems properly to belong.

But, still, the Disciples are "an off-shoot of the Sandemanian sect of Scotland," writes Prof. Whitsitt, with imperturbable gravity. It seems necessary to look at this affirmation more narrowly than we have hitherto done. First of all, let us ask, what, in such a connection, does the word "offshoot?" imply? It may be well to let Noah Webster answer this question. His definition is exceedingly clear:

"Offshoot, n. (from *off* and *shoot.)* That which shoots off or separates from a main stem or channel; as the *offshoots* of a tree: 'The *offshoots* of the Gulf stream.' J.D. Forbes."

This cannot be improved upon by lexicographic skill. It is perfect on the very surface. But in the light of it, let us look at Prof. Whitsitt's historical dictum. Were the Disciples ever connected with the Sandemanian sect, or any branch of such sect? Never, never! Thomas and Alexander Campbell were in the beginning, Presbyterians of the very strictest persuasion, nor had they departed widely from their ancestral traditions up to the day of their immersion by a regularly ordained Baptist preacher. Sometime after that event, the church of which they were members was formally received into the fellowship of the Redstone association of Baptists, within the geographical limits of which it was located. As a simple matter of historical fact, they remained in connection with the Baptist people as long as they were permitted to do so. Touching the cause of their separation, I need say nothing here. But I may be allowed to say, in passing, that the founding of a distinct people was no part of their plan. They did not judge it desirable, however calmly they accepted the inevitable, when it came. They wanted no new order. There were divisions enough already. They deprecated what might seem to the world like the formation of a new sect. Their whole end and purpose was anti-sectarian from the very beginning. They may not have been always wise, for that is not given to men in the flesh. But of their general soundness of judgment on New Testament questions, and their honest intent to serve the great interests of truth and righteousness, there is no reason to doubt. If men will be just, not partisan, to this conclusion must they come at last. There have indeed been large-minded Baptists, in later times (perhaps not many, but still some), who have thought that a satisfactory *modus vivendi* was not impossible, and that with a more generous toleration on the part of the Baptists than was common in those days, there need have been no division at all. Upon these questions I need not enter. They matter nothing, here or there, in the present investigation. Nor do the Disciples make any complaint today, however it may have been when the ties of love and fellowship were being rudely sundered by what they then regarded as a most unchristian intolerance. Our fathers accepted the situation, because they could not help themselves, albeit unwillingly, and we now regard it as having been Providential. We shall perform our much-needed work in the world, under God, far more effectively than we could have done, in the face of obstructive tactics, in any ecclesiastical connection with the Baptists. The day is sure to come when it will be otherwise; but it is scarcely here yet. God grant it may not be far distant. But if the chronicles of those tumultuous times have correctly reached us, our fathers, as I have said, did not go out of their own accord. They would fain have suffered much, rather than cut loose from dear fellow-shoots in Christ, and set adrift from their old ecclesiastical moorings. They did not *shoot off* at all; they were *driven off.* True, the Mahoning association, to which the Campbells belonged, when the separation was actually taking place, may be said to have gone bodily into the reform movement. But it had been a regular Baptist association. This is not disputed. Nor was any considerable section of the Disciples ever in connection with the Sandemanians. Individuals doubtless came into the movement from Sandemanian congregations, as there were those who came into it from all denominations,

Catholic and Protestant. Leaders among the Scotch Baptists, and Scotch Baptist churches, whether in the old world or new, would more naturally seek fellowship and association with the Disciples than with their American cousins of the Baptist name, whenever they could be persuaded to surrender the straight-laced Calvinism in which they had been reared, because, in the matter of organization and worship, they were sure of a more sympathetic reception. Doubtless such affiliations took place, not infrequently, in the earlier years of our history as a distinct people. But as a mere matter of fact, the Disciples were never in ecclesiastic connection with any Sandemanian party, and could not possibly, therefore, have *shot off* from "the Sandemanian sect."

The truth is, we are not an offshoot at all. As a people in mutual fellowship, we have been gathered from all quarters of the great Babel of modern sectdom by the acceptance of the most catholic and Christian basis of fellowship that the world has known since the rise of the original apostasy. We feel ourselves able to make this affirmation good in any forum, and in the face of any foe. But of this even we do not boast. We have nothing that we have not received from God, and to him we give the glory. Paul is nothing, Apollos is nothing, God, the giver of all good, is alone entitled to the praise. We are not an "offshoot" from any sect. The Campbells came to our present ground from the Presbyterians, by way of the Baptists. B.W. Stone, and hosts of others, came from the Presbyterians, through the "old Christian" movement. John T. Johnson, John Smith, (and there has only been one John Smith after all), the Mortons, Creaths, and multitudes of others, great and small, came out, or were cast out, from the Associated Baptists, because they could not rest content with the fellowship of a narrow sect, when they felt the uplifting power of Christ's prayer for the unity of his people in the holy communion of a universal Christian brotherhood. God have mercy on those who could so rest content! It is to be told to the eternal honor of the men I have named, that they belonged not to that class. There is no people on earth today, who are so clearly no "offshoot," as Webster defines the word, from any sect that ever existed, as the Disciples of Christ — according to Prof. Whitsitt, "more commonly called Campbellites!"

There had been, as in every other movement of great magnitude and enduring character, a long period of preparation. The souls of men had been anxiously studying the most vital problems of the common faith, and the current teaching had no solution to offer which could be accepted as satisfactory. The usual presentations of the way of life and salvation were far removed from the simplicity and tangibility of the New Testament period. The ready appropriation of Christ as Savior, which was so marked a feature of the apostolic era, had been lost utterly. Men were groping their ways in darkness, where at first all had been light and blessedness. They found themselves bewildered by subtle distinctions impossible to minds untrained in religious metaphysics. On one side of them was the bane of formalism, and on the other the upas of mysticism. For the basis of their personal assurance of salvation, they had been compelled to fall back on emotional experiences, which sober common sense — whenever they gave it free and honest play — told them were quite as untrustworthy as the fantastic stuff of which dreams are made. No wonder they felt themselves impelled to seek after the "old paths," that they might find once more the peace which in the hearts of the first Christians, had been an ever-flowing river. If Glas and Sandeman and McLean were among the leaders who sought relief from current perplexities in speculation, and current phantasms of experience, by a thorough study, *de novo,* of the apostolic gospel, and the spiritual life of the first Christians, then there is no higher title to enduring honor in the kingdom of heaven than that to which they may lay humble, but honest claim. It is to be frankly conceded that, to some extent at least, this honor is due to them. And in so far as they may have contributed, however indirectly, to shape the most fruitful movement of our modern period, the day of eternity will decree them full reward. Heaven forbid that we should claim for the Campbells, and Stones, and Johnsons, and Smiths, of our own day, the honor which rightfully belongs to others. If Alexander Campbell built upon a foundation which other men had laid, let him have simply the credit which is his due. But truth is no more divine, no less effectual to salvation, whether McLean or Campbell first brought it to the light again, in these ends of the ages. If Sandeman and McLean saw what truth they did see but dimly, it should not be thought strange. If Campbell saw more truth, and saw it more clearly, it does not make him greater or better than they. Truth has always made its way through difficulties, and its celestial shape has never greeted the eyes of men, save through the mists and fogs which evermore enwrap our nether world. If Sandeman or McLean is the real leader to whom our divine movement owes its origin, be it so. Who cares? This is not especially a question of whom, but of what? Not who began the work, humanly speaking, but, is it of God? Save for this single question, we care not a farthing. If our origin could really be traced in fairness to Robert Sandeman, it would not give us a moment's concern. Who is Sandeman? Who is Campbell? All truth is of God; and whether Sandeman or Campbell proclaim it,

God's truth shall stand forever. This is simply a question of priority in discovery. It has, at most, that value, and not a scruple more. Please let all the Whitsitt's in the world understand how little the issue they have raised affects our confidence in the truth we plead. We hold it, and plead it, not because it is from Campbell, or is supposed by some partisan to have been advocated by Sandeman, but because it is from God, and shall stand the ordeal of the last day!

CHAPTER III:
A HISTORICAL SKETCH

It is not proposed to follow our author into the minute, and, for the most part, insignificant matters of detail, into which he has seen fit to enter at great length; in the first place, because a discussion of these details is not needed, and, in the second place, because the purpose I have in view may be better accomplished in another way. An independent statement of the chief historical points preliminary to our discussion will be more satisfactory to seekers after truth than an examination, *seriatim*, of statements, often unimportant, and, generally irrelevant to the main issue.

"No man," says Paul, "liveth or dieth to himself." We are inseparable parts of a total humanity, in spite of individual self-assertion within narrow limits. No man has ever lived whose character and achievements were not determined, to a great extent, by the conditions in the midst of which his individual lot was cast. We cannot wholly escape our environment, though we exert ourselves ever so strenuously. The cultivated man of today is indeed the heir of all the ages. The great tides of life and thought come rushing in upon us from the past, and we cannot shut them off, if we would. Even that which is peculiar to us as individuals, that which we bring with us into the world, has been shaping itself through centuries of varied experience, along the almost infinitely extended lines of our personal ancestry. Apart from all possible inferences, these facts are simply undeniable. Luther, Calvin, Wesley, Campbell and all the world's great leaders, have been as much under the molding influence of this great divine law as the men supposed to have been made of more common clay.

We go, therefore, to the prevailing tendencies, to the great controlling drifts of religious thought among the dissenting Protestants of Great Britain, in the latter half of the eighteenth century, that we may discover what were the influences in the midst of which Alexander Campbell was born and educated, and determine how far his individual development was molded by these influences, and also to what extent they contributed to give shape and character to the movement which was the inspiration of his remarkable life. I have said "dissenting Protestants," because the intellectual currents in the established church were somewhat different, and, in any event, have little to do with the subject before us.

Among dissenters, especially those known, in a general way, as Independents, whether Baptist or Pedo-baptist, the period I have indicated was eminently formative. There were sharp discussions, tinged sometimes with bitterness, but the various influences and counter-influences were at work, which ultimately imparted to them the theological trend and ecclesiastical forms that characterize, in the main, their descendants at the present time. In this period, Sandeman, Booth, Fuller, and McLean touched the high-water mark of their intellectual activity. At the same time also, John Wesley was at the height of his wonderful career. And although his influence lay, for the most part, rather outside the lines of progress which mainly concern our inquiry, yet, indirectly, the religious thought of all sections of the Island, and all types of thinkers, were more or less affected. We cannot afford, therefore, to leave him wholly out of this brief survey.

Among the questions of special significance in this period, the most important, theologically, as I have already intimated, was that concerning the nature of "saving faith." But closely related to this, and scarcely less important to our present investigation, was a question as to the theological ground on which faith becomes the principle of justification under the gospel. Let us seek briefly to get at the very pith of these old-time controversies. Let us lose sight, if we can, of any bearing which our historical facts may have on present issues, or the theological standing of parties to present issues, for only thus shall we attain to that judicial impartiality which this investigation imperatively demands. Truth is everything, party is nothing.

To begin with John Wesley.

He was, as the reader is presumed to know a member of the Established Church of England. Early in life, he was greatly exercised over the indifference and impiety, not only of the laity of the Establishment, but of the very ministers of the sanctuary itself. He was thus led to organize, at Oxford, a little society, having for its object the promotion of godliness. This society soon came to be spoken of among the irreligious as "Wesley's godly club," and Prof. Whitsitt lends his sanction to this sneer — let us hope unintentionally — in referring to it by that designation. Afterwards Wesley went as a missionary to Georgia along with Gen. Oglethorpe, the founder of that colony. On the voyage out the vessel in which he sailed encountered a terrible storm, and Wesley, though an ordained priest in the Established Church, became greatly frightened. In the same company were some Moravian missionaries, whose superior calmness greatly impressed him. Naturally, he was led to suspect some defect in his religious life, though it does not appear that any change took place in his religious views or experiences until after he had returned to England. Meantime, however, he had laid the foundation of his great life-work in America. Among his acquaintances at Oxford at this period was Peter Bohler, a Moravian preacher. Charles Wesley had undertaken to teach Bohler the English language, and Peter, to repay one favor with another, straightway proceeded to teach Charles the Moravian theology. This was about the 20th of February, 1738. On the 21st day of May, Whitsunday, Charles Wesley "obtained the sense of adoption," whatever that may mean (for the New Testament furnishes no equivalent expression), and "just one week later," as a trustworthy chronicler tells us, "his brother John obtained the same blessing." We are further informed that "Bohler, aided by the testimony of several living witnesses, convinced him that to gain peace of mind he must renounce that dependence upon his own works which had hitherto been the bane of his experience, and replace it with a full reliance on the blood of Christ shed for him." At a Moravian society meeting in Aldersgate Street, while one was reading Luther's statement of the change which God works in the heart through faith, Wesley himself says, "I felt my heart strangely warmed. I felt I did trust in Christ alone for salvation; and an assurance was given me, that he had taken away *my* sin, even *mine*, and saved *me* from the law of sin and death." These words deserve special attention. They show us that the notion of a sensuous revelation of pardon, considered as an element of saving faith, came to John Wesley, and through him to Methodism, from the Moravian mystics. One cannot help wondering what would have been the effect upon the movement we now call Methodism, if Wesley's course had been wrought out free from contact with the excellent, but highly imaginative people. To Wesley himself, this Aldersgate Street experience was conversion to Christ. Before that time he had not known Christ as his Savior. From this conviction, I presume, he never wavered. It would be interesting to know how many Methodist preachers so understand it today. Had John Wesley died before that notable event in his life, what would have been his fate? Ah! Well! Let us hope that everyone sees things more clearly now. God grant it may be so!

It was a member of Mr. Wesley's Oxford Society, James Hervey, as Prof. Whitsitt correctly informs us, that wrote the "Dialogues between Theron and Aspasio." The leading feature of this work was the setting forth of the Methodist-Moravian conception of saving faith, and the experimental processes through which "the sense of adoption is obtained. To this work of Hervey, Robert Sandeman replied. He took the ground of the Westminster divines, but went further, bravely insisting not only that "assurance is not inseparable from saving faith," but that it is really no part of saving faith, in any case. That is, the faith which saves, and the assurance of salvation, are distinct in consciousness, and that the latter necessarily depends on the former. Or, in other words, the consciousness of faith in Christ is the prior condition of conscious salvation. This I give as the substance, without caring to quote words. To the extent here stated, Abraham Booth, apparently, and Andrew Fuller, certainly, agreed with him. It is necessary to bear this in mind, for Prof. Whitsitt, seemingly, would make the impression that while the Scotch Baptists, whom he treats as Sandemanians pure and simple, agreed with Sandeman regarding the *nature* of faith, other Baptists did not. But Fuller and Sandeman did not differ on the *nature* of faith. On this question they agreed perfectly. They differed of course about other matters, but the agreement concerning the nature of faith must not be lost sight of, if we would have a clear view of the historic situation.

Fuller and McLean

Now, among Baptists of the eighteenth century no name is more justly held in veneration than that of Andrew Fuller. To this all Baptists agree. He was in fact the leader of progressive Baptists in England, just as McLean was easily leader of the Baptists of Scotland. The exact differences between these distinguished men, as representing differences between two sections of the Baptist church militant, in their day, become important to us here, on account of their relation to the chief question which Prof. Whitsitt has raised. And as McLean confessedly agreed with Sandeman in the controversies regarding faith, I shall draw on him for what information is needed on that side of the question. Prof. Whitsitt will not object to this. Our comparison, therefore, will be between McLean and Fuller. In the first place, we shall hear Fuller, the Baptist *par excellence*, as he is regarded among American Baptists today.

In his preface to his "*Gospel Worthy of All Acceptation*," Mr. Fuller tells us that "he had formerly held different sentiments" from those advocated in that book. For years, however, he had been in doubt. These doubts had arisen chiefly from thinking upon certain passages of Scripture which seemed clearly to imply that repentance and faith are the "immediate duty" of all men to whom the gospel offer of salvation comes. This is the main thesis of his book, and his statement, on its very face, shows the Antinomian tendencies which he had formerly cherished. But besides the Scripture texts, the reading of the labors of Elliot,

Brainerd, and others, who had been eminently successful among the American Indians, had greatly impressed him. Like the apostles, the work of these men seemed to be plain before them. In their addresses to these benighted heathen, they seemed to have none of the difficulties with which he felt himself encumbered. That is to say, he had been a very narrow Calvinist, and his theories of inability, passive regeneration, limited atonement, etc., had been in his way. Besides, he had regarded appropriation as being of the very essence of saving faith, so that, without a sort of special revelation, no one could be a true believer; or indeed had a warrant to believe. But slowly he was beginning to see light. For four years he wrestled with his doubts, disclosing them to no one. "Once in company with a minister, whom he greatly respected" (could he have been a Sandemanian minister?), "it was thrown out as a matter of inquiry, 'Whether we had generally entertained just notions concerning unbelief.' It was common to speak of unbelief as a calling in question the truth of our personal religion; whereas, he remarked, 'It was the calling in question the truth of what God had said.'" "This remark," Fuller says, "seemed to carry in it its own evidence." Pending questions of "origins" and "offshoots," we cannot but regret that the name of this sensible minister has been withheld from us. Alexander Campbell once intimated a suspicion that Fuller had learned the best things he knew from the Sandemanians, and though Fuller tells us that at this time he had not read Sandeman's writings, it is not at all impossible that the excellent minister in question had both read them, and profited by them. In any event, the incident here recorded let the first glimmer of the new light into Fuller's soul. From the point of view thus attained, "his thoughts," he tells us, "began to enlarge." He preached upon the subject "more than once." Finally, he began "to consider faith as *a persuasion of the truth of what God hath said*." He was "aware that the generality of Christians with whom he was acquainted viewed *the belief of the gospel* as something pre-supposed in faith, rather than as being of the essence of it; and considered the contrary as the opinion of Mr. Robert Sandeman, which they were agreed in regarding as favorable to a dead or inoperative kind of faith. At this time, as I said a moment since, Mr. Fuller assures us he had read none of Sandeman's works. Afterwards he read both Sandeman and McLean, and says expressly that he was in "accord with them in considering the belief of the gospel as saving faith," but that he and they attached different ideas to "believing." Concerning these differences, we shall see clearly before we are through this examination. It is sufficient here, if the reader notes distinctly, that as regards the *nature* of faith,

Fuller says plainly that he was in accord with Sandeman and McLean. (See preface to Fuller's Gospel, *passim*, and also appendix to sixth American edition, Page 168, where he says in so many words: "I have the pleasure to agree with Mr. McLean in considering the belief of the gospel as saving faith. Our disagreement on this subject is confined to the question, *What the belief of the gospel includes?*" It is clear therefore, that Fuller, Sandeman and McLean, were in entire accord on the nature of faith, and we may proceed at once to other items of interest. It is worthwhile, however, to note briefly, in passing, the steps by which Mr. Fuller seems to have reached his conclusion, *"that faith is the persuasion of the truth of what God hath said."* He expressly tells us he had "felt himself encumbered with difficulties" while holding another view. This statement surely ought to surprise no one, and can surprise no one who has thoughtfully considered what it involves. It seems to lie on the surface of the New Testament, that repentance and faith are the immediate duty of all men on hearing the gospel. But the duty to believe implies, of course, a divine warrant, and also that there is nothing in the nature of faith to make the performance of the duty impossible. A warrant to believe means the universality of the atonement, and the *natural ability* of the sinner to accept it. Fuller still held the doctrine of the sinner's *moral inability* to repent and believe, but his theological scheme took slight account of it. The ground of such inability was in man's sinful nature, in the obliquity of his will, and the aversion of his heart to God, and hence his unbelief was his own fault. If there is natural ability — that is, if there are the *natural faculties* which make faith possible, after the sinful disposition has been removed by divine grace — it is a sufficient basis for the obligation to believe. It does not matter that this sinful disposition comes from inherited depravity, and that it reaches back to the fall of Adam, for though the sinner may have lost his ability to obey, God has not lost his right to command. But Fuller saw clearly enough, that, if faith contains in its own essence the assurance of a personal interest in Christ, it cannot he the sinner's duty to believe, until the knowledge of salvation has been bestowed. So he rejected the doctrine of Hervey and "the generality of Christians with whom he was acquainted," and accepted the only view of faith which seemed to him to be consistent with the sinner's obligation to believe. In this final outcome of his reasoning, he was unquestionably right, however cloudy his speculations in regard to the difference between natural and moral ability may seem to us, in the clearer light of our own time.

Fuller, Sandeman, and McLean, were also in complete accord regarding the necessity of a special divine influence in order to enable the sinner to believe. The differences among them concerning "what is included in believing" did not affect this particular at all. The proof here is ample, and, I presume, will not be denied. I therefore pass on.

The differences which we have to note begin at this point.

Sandeman and McLean held that faith, in its last analysis, is the mind's acceptance of "God's testimony concerning his Son," and that holiness of disposition is the *effect* of faith. Fuller, on his part, unable to escape entirely from the influence of his earlier view, maintained, that the implantation of a principle of holiness "is antecedent to faith, and thus included in it, as a part of its essence. " Briefly, the difference in our style of speaking is this: According to Fuller, change of heart takes place before faith — is, indeed, the one condition without which faith is impossible — while Sandeman and McLean insisted strenuously that holiness of heart is secured only *through* faith. In other words, the difference is that between antecedent and consequent; between cause, in a certain sense, and effect. It is not to be maintained that these distinctions amount to nothing, or that general unanimity has, even now, been attained in regard to them. It may be thought that they are of little practical account, and plain Christians, devoted mainly to questions of organization and work, will be inclined, no doubt, to pass them by as unimportant; but as long as the human mind insists on having a rational and symmetrical representation of the truth it holds, all the more thoughtful disciples of the Lord will see the necessity of giving to such questions due importance in their scheme of religious thought.

If regeneration be the same thing as a change of heart (which has been generally held by the so-styled Evangelical denominations), then Fuller's theology places regeneration before faith; while, according to Sandeman and McLean, regeneration is *through* faith, and therefore, after it. Baptists, today, for the most part, stand on Fuller's ground, but the Disciples, without exception reject it as anti-scriptural and irrational. Of this there is no pretense of denial, whatever inferences men like Mr. Whitsitt may see fit to draw from it. But while the "generality" of Baptists adopt Fuller's doctrine of the necessity of "a holy principle in order to believing," few of them, I am persuaded, will accept, without great qualification, his definition of saving faith. The fact is, our modern Baptists are still with Hervey and the Methodists in their view of that question. The logically impossible theory which Fuller gave up for what Dr. Clifford has recently styled a better "working theology," is still maintained among them with essential unanimity. What Baptist preacher now speaks of faith as "the persuasion of the truth of what God has revealed?" Or who among them has been known to define it as "the belief of the gospel?" And yet among the English Baptists of the latter half of the last century, this was Fuller's most characteristic contention. He boldly took this ground when "the generality of Christians with whom he was acquainted" rejected it as the doctrine of Robert Sandeman. On this question our modern Baptists are not Fullerites. The fact is, they hold with remarkable unanimity that "the sense of adoption," save in very rare cases, is the real test of saving faith. It is to this test that the applicant for church membership is, in the first place, invariably subjected. Failing here, he may not be positively rejected, but his "experience" is certain to be regarded as defective at the most vital point. Oh, for another Fuller to lead them quite out of the wilderness in whose depths they are still wandering!

But besides the matter here considered, there were certain differences concerning the ground upon which faith justifies, which seem to demand some notice in our present survey. In any possible view of the matter, faith is, so to say, the act — if one may call it an act — of the creature. It is the sinner that believes, not God. And no view of enabling grace that one may hold in the least affects this conclusion. Say, if the reader chooses, that faith is the gift of God — a position which was not in debate among the men whose views we are looking into — and it still remains true, that the sinner, being divinely enabled, "believes the gospel," or "accepts the testimony of God concerning Christ." Now this faith, which is undeniably the sinner's own act, either has in it, or has not, the element of *holiness;* it contains, or does not contain, in itself, intrinsic moral or spiritual value. But if faith contains in itself holiness, how is justification by faith a gracious justification? For in such case, a holy principle in the sinner is made the basis of his justification. So reasoned McLean, and Fuller replied as best he could. McLean pressed the difficulty upon him with great vigor and effect. I take no side in their controversy. They were able men, but they were both in the fog. That my readers may have a clear view of this old-time discussion, I beg leave to offer a few extracts for their consideration. As a specimen of theological dialectics, a hundred years ago, it cannot fail to interest them.

> *This knowledge and belief of the truth as it is in Jesus, although a duty incumbent on all who hear the gospel, is nevertheless the special gift of God, being the effect of divine teaching by means of the Word, and peculiar to the elect; so that whatever appearances*

there may be of it in false professors, they have not at bottom the same perception of truth, nor that persuasion of it upon its proper evidence which real believers have. But as we cannot discern the difference by the confession of the mouth, when that confession accords with the form of sound words, it is therefore necessary that true faith should be distinguished by its general effects upon the heart and life.

As to its effects upon the heart, such is the important, interesting and salutary nature of the truth testified in the gospel, with its suitableness and freeness for the chief of sinners, that it is no sooner perceived and believed, than it takes possession of the will and affections, and becomes in the soul the ground of its hope, trust and reliance; the object of its desire, acceptance, esteem and joy; and the principle of every holy, active, and gracious disposition of the heart.

But these effects of faith, or which is the same, of the truth believed, ought not to be confounded with faith itself, as is commonly done. Though faith is the confidence of things hoped for, and also worketh by love; yet it is neither hope nor love, for the apostle distinguished it from both. And now abideth faith, hope, and love — these three. The same may be said of its other effects upon the heart, for whatever is more than belief is more than faith, and ought to go by another name.

It will, perhaps be asked, why so nice in distinguishing here? What harm can arise from including in the nature of faith such holy dispositions, affections and exercises of heart, as are confessedly inseparable from it? In answer to this, let it be considered.

1. That unless we carefully distinguish faith from its effects, particularly on the point of a sinner's acceptance with God, the important doctrine of free justification by faith alone, will be materially affected. The Scriptures pointedly declare that God justifies freely by his grace, through the redemption that is in Christ Jesus; and that this justification is received through faith in Christ's blood. Faith in this case is always distinguished from, and opposed to, the works of the law; not merely of the ceremonial law which was peculiar to the Jews, but of that law by which is the knowledge of sin, which says Thou shalt not covet, and which requires not only outward good actions, but love, and every good disposition of heart, both towards God and our neighbor; so that the works of the law respect the heart as well as life. The distinc-

tion, therefore, between faith and works, on this subject, is not that which is between inward and outward conformity to the law; for if faith is not in this case, distinguished from and opposed to our conformity to the law, both outwardly and inwardly, it cannot be said that we are 'justified by faith without the deeds of the law,' or that God "justified the ungodly." Faith indeed, as a principle of action, "worketh by love;" but it is not as thus working that it is "imputed for righteousness;" for it is expressly declared that "righteousness is imputed to him that worketh not, but believeth on him that justifieth the ungodly." It is of faith that it might be by grace; and grace and works are represented as being incompatible with each other; for to him that worketh the reward is not reckoned of grace, but of debt.

Now when men include in the very nature of justifying faith, such good dispositions, holy affections, and pious exercises of heart as the moral law requires, and so make them necessary (no matter under what consideration) to a sinner's acceptance with God, it perverts the gospel doctrine on this important subject, and makes justification to be at least, as it were, by the works of the law." — McLean on The Commission, Cincinnati, 1871, Pages 72-74.

The reader will easily note the points here made, (a) Faith is the special gift of God. (b) It is peculiar to the elect, (c) It is distinguished by its genuine effects upon the heart and life, (d) But these effects are, in point of fact, inseparable from it — *i.e.* they always follow it immediately, (e) They must not, however, be confounded with it, as is commonly done. "Whatever is more than belief, is more than faith, and ought to go by another name." (f) Especially is faith to be distinguished from its effects in the matter of justification, for if faith is held to include, in its nature, holiness of disposition, the sinner is accepted on the ground of such holiness, and justification by faith is no longer justification by grace, but to all intents and purposes, justification by law, or by works, (g) Further, it could not be said in that case that "He justifieth the ungodly," for faith is supposed to include a godly state of the heart. These points are, of course, keenly made, but it is easy to see how much, and how little, such speculations had to do with the "origin of the Disciples of Christ."

Andrew Fuller, as has been said, took a very different ground. We must also allow him to speak for himself.

"I have the pleasure." says Fuller, *"to agree with Mr. McLean in considering the belief of the gospel as saving faith. Our disagreement on this subject, is confined to the question: '**What the belief of the gospel includes.**' Mr. M. so explains it, as to carefully exclude every exercise of the heart or will, as either included in it, or having any influence upon it. Whatever of this exists in a believer, he considers as belonging to the **effects** of faith, rather than to faith itself. If I understand him, he pleads for such a belief of the gospel, as has nothing in it of a holy nature, nothing of conformity to the moral law 'in heart or life;' a **passive** reception of truth, in which the will has no concern; and this, because it is opposed **to the works of the law** in the article of justification. On this ground, he accounts for the apostle's language in Rom. 4:5: 'To him that worketh not, but believeth on Him that justifieth the **ungodly,**' understanding by the terms, 'he that worketh not,' one who has done nothing yet which is pleasing to God; and by the term 'ungodly,' one that is actually an enemy to God.* (It must be remembered that Mr. Fuller is here saying how he understands McLean. Whether he understood him correctly, or not, the reader will judge from the words of M., himself, as quoted above.)

*If Mr. M. had only affirmed that faith is opposed to works, even to every good disposition of the heart, as the **ground of acceptance with God;** that we are not justified by it **as a work**; or that whatever moral goodness it may possess, it is not **as such** that it is imputed to us for righteousness, there had been no dispute between us. But this distinction he rejects... He is not contented with faith being opposed to works in point of justification; it must also be opposed to them in its own nature. In short, if there be any possibility of drawing a certain conclusion from what a writer, in almost every form of speech, has advanced, it must be concluded that he means to deny that there is anything holy in the nature of faith; and that could it be separated from its effects, as he supposes it is in justification, it would leave the person who possessed it, among the enemies of God... Mr. M. allows faith to be a **duty** — it is 'the command of God' and a 'part of obedience to God' — that to believe what God says is **right**, and that unbelief, which is its opposite, is a 'great and heinous sin.' But how can these things agree? If there be nothing of the exercise of a holy disposition in what is **commanded** of God, in what is **right**, and in what is an exercise of **obedience**; by what rule are we to judge of what is holy and what is* *not? I can scarcely conceive of a truth more self-evident than this, 'That God's commands extend only to that which comes under the influence of the will.' Knowledge can be no further a duty, nor ignorance a sin, than each is influenced by the moral state of the heart; and the same is true of faith and unbelief. To receive truth into the **heart**, indeed, is duty; for this is voluntary acquiescence in it; but that in which the will has no concern, cannot possibly be so. "* Fuller's Gospel, Sixth American edition, Cincinatti, O., 1832. Appendix. Pages 165-170.

I cannot afford space for further extracts; nor is it necessary. The gist of the debate, and the main positions of the disputants, are apparent enough from what I have given. I hope no reader has felt a weariness stealing over him, as he has sought to follow these champions in their conflict over issues, which, in their 18th century form, are not now heard of at all. They are not without interest, however, as showing important points of connection in the continuous development of religious thought.

It is important to our inquiry that the precise position of the parties to these old issues shall be distinctly understood. How far Fuller and McLean agreed, and precisely wherein they differed, may not be entitled to the least weight in determining what is true or false, in our discussion of doctrines at the present time, but, if the question relate to an influence exerted, or *said* to have been exerted, upon the mind of Mr. Campbell, and through him upon the Disciples of Christ, by these half-forgotten conflicts, they straightway become interesting to us. It is on this account, solely, that I have asked the attention of my readers to the details which have been thus far presented; and for the same reason I must solicit their indulgence while I seek to throw still more light upon the subject. I prefer to risk the charge of tediousness, rather than that of obscurity, on any vital point.

It cannot be without interest to us to note the fact that when Fuller speaks of *repentance* and *faith*, he uniformly places the words in this order, while McLean adopts the contrary order of *faith* and *repentance*. It would doubtless be a great mistake to suppose that the naked question of the order in which faith and repentance take place in the sinner's return to God was regarded by either of these distinguished men as a matter of special importance. There is no reason why it should have been so considered. The truth is, that the way of speaking which we here observe has a much deeper significance. It goes, indeed, to the very roots of rival theologies. With Fuller, as we have seen, faith was always the act of a regenerate soul. For while he insisted that it was the sinner's immediate duty to believe, he, at the same time, firmly maintained that it was impossible for him to do so, until the obstructing hindrance of native depravity had been removed. This is the sole meaning of his contention for the necessity of a *principle of holiness in order to believing*. Faith is only possible to a renewed heart. The implantation of a holy disposition precedes it in every case. Naturally, he thought repentance would be the first expression of this new principle of holiness, even though the subject might not himself be conscious of its priority. In *"The Gospel Worthy of all Acceptation"* — Sixth American edition, Cincinnati, 1832 — we have the following statement and illustration:

> *That the bias of the heart requires to be turned to God, antecedent to believing, has been admitted, because the nature of believing is such that it cannot be exercised while the soul is under the dominion of willful blindness, hardness, and aversion. These dispositions are represented in the Scriptures as a bar in the way of faith, as being inconsistent with it; and which, consequently, require to be taken out of the way. But whatever necessity there may be for a change of heart in order to believing, it is neither necessary nor possible that the party should be conscious of it till he has believed. It is necessary that the eyes of a blind man should be opened before he can see, but it is neither necessary nor possible for him to know that his eyes are open till he doth see. It is only by surrounding objects appearing to his view, that he knows the obstructing film to be removed.*

This is in reply to a Mr. Brine, who, while agreeing with Fuller that regeneration or change of heart precedes faith, argues there from that only the regenerate have a warrant to believe. To set this aside, Fuller says in effect, that though it be indeed true that regeneration precedes faith, it is no more possible for the party to be conscious of his regeneration till he believes, than for a blind man to know that his eyes have been opened before he is conscious of seeing. Faith is the soul's seeing, and regeneration is the removal of the film from the soul's eyes.

Again: (*Appendix* pp. 214-215)

> *All I contend for is, that it is not by means of a spiritual perception, or belief of the gospel, that the heart is, for the first time, effectually influenced towards God: for spiritual perception and belief are represented as the **effects**, and not as the causes of such influence.*
>
> *A spiritual perception of the glory of some things appears to be*

the first sensation of which the mind is conscious; but it is not the first operation of God upon it.

It is clear, therefore, that in the strict theological sense, Fuller placed regeneration before faith; as the removal of the film from a blind man's eyes necessarily precedes the act of seeing. But as regards repentance and faith, he says expressly, that "saying faith *implies* repentance;" *i.e.,* repentance, in the order of Christian experience, comes before faith. *Appendix*, p. 179.

So his theology stood thus: (1) Regeneration; (2) Repentance; (3) Faith. This may seem strange when we remember that he defined faith as "the belief of the gospel;" or as *"the persuasion of the truth of what God hath said."* But there can be no doubt that such was his view, though we may totally fail to see how he could obviate, in his own mind, the difficulties which it involves. Great men are not always consistent with themselves, to say nothing of their want of consistency with truth seen clearly by other people.

While, therefore, there can be no debate as to the view maintained by Fuller, it is quite as certain that McLean held the directly opposite position. With the former, a change of heart was thought to precede any real "belief of the gospel;" while the latter strenuously insisted, that *repentance,* and all *holy dispositions*, were to be regarded as the *effects* of such belief. It is this single feature of their protracted debates, which has descended, as a living issue, to the Christian thinkers of today. The sharp controversy between these men, and the schools to which they belonged, concerning the ground on which faith is accounted for righteousness, whether holy dispositions were to be excluded from the nature of faith in order that justification might be an act of sovereign grace, and all kindred contentions, are no longer in debate anywhere. To all well informed people, this goes with the saying. Argument is unnecessary. But Fuller's opponents met him with the objection that regeneration before faith, implies the contradiction of a *godly unbeliever.* "A spiritual perception of the glory of divine things," says Fuller, "is the first sensation of which the mind is conscious, but it is not the first operation of God upon it." Of this first operation, regeneration is the immediate effect, and faith is the effect of regeneration. The consciousness of faith, so to say, reveals the fact of regeneration, as a prior work of the Spirit. But, if this be the order of experience, it is impossible to say certainly that regeneration may not be separated from faith by an interval of time. In any event, if a holy disposition precedes faith, *godliness* comes first, and *faith* afterwards. On the other hand, the retort was read, that, if all holy dispositions must be excluded from faith, as not of its essence, and, in point of fact, not co-existent with it, at the moment of justification, then, this theory gives the equal absurdity of an *ungodly believer.* McLean insisted most strenuously that the justification of the *ungodly* (which Paul expressly teaches,) implies that the act of justification attaches to faith in advance of the holy dispositions which follow it. In this case, who can say that the theory is not open to the charge brought against it? Does it not involve the contradiction, momentarily, at least, of an *ungodly believer?* Looking back at this discussion, from our present point of view, it seems safe to say that each of these theologians succeeded in overturning, in part, his opponent's theory. Both were right, and both were wrong; but in a different way. Fuller was wrong in maintaining the priority of regeneration to faith, and McLean was equally wrong in arguing that a gracious justification excludes all holy dispositions from the soul, at the moment when God justifies. It is strange that so acute a thinker should have been bewildered by the mere logic of the letter, in a matter which now seems so clear. To do equal justice, it must be said that Fuller did not admit that, in ordinary cases, faith is separated from regeneration in time, nor did McLean teach that the holy dispositions which proceed from faith, are separated from it in consciousness. "The priority contended for," says Fuller, "is rather in the order of nature than of time." "And if there be a priority in the order of time, owing to the want of opportunity of knowing the truth, yet when a person embraces Christ so far as he has the means of knowing him, he is in effect a believer." On the other hand McLean says expressly, that *"the saving truth testified in the gospel, is no sooner perceived and believed than it takes possession of the will and affections, and becomes in the soul the ground of its hope, reliance, and the principle of every holy, active and gracious disposition of the heart."*

It must be admitted, I think, that Fuller's doctrine of regeneration before faith is inconsistent with his definition of faith. For if faith be "the persuasion of the truth of what God hath said," it is the necessary condition of all saving influences exerted by means of the gospel. Whatever precedes the "belief of the gospel," is accomplished without the gospel. If regeneration precedes "the belief of the gospel," then the gospel is not the means of regeneration, and all those passages of Scripture which teach the instrumentality of God's word in regeneration, are rendered void and unmeaning. It seems clear that most Baptists now perceive Fuller's inconsistency at this point, for they have given up his view of the nature of faith. They do not teach that faith is "the persuasion of the truth of what God hath said;" nor do they define faith as "the belief of the gospel." They are not satisfied to regard faith as the root of good dispositions, and the mainspring of all holy and gracious activities, nor do they recognize the dominant element of intellectual conviction, which the Scriptures everywhere give to it, but, on the contrary, resolve it, in effect, into a mere emotional experience, from which, the scriptural idea of *belief* has been well-nigh eliminated. Besides this, as I intimated above, they have practically gone back to the doctrine of faith against which all Fuller's writings were an earnest and vehement protest. Like Wesley, they regard an emotional consciousness of pardon as the very essence of true faith. The point evermore insisted upon, in judging of conversion, is the *feeling* testimony of the forgiveness of sins. "Do you, my brother or sister, *feel* that God, for Christ's sake, has pardoned *you*?" is a question never omitted. It is not the consciousness of faith so much as the mystic sense of salvation, which is the uniform criterion of judgment, when the church with open doors sits for reception of converts into its pale. This is consistent with Wesleyanism, and Moravianism, or even with the Antinomianism from which Fuller vainly sought to deliver them, but it is inconsistent with Fullers most characteristic contention, and utterly inconsistent with the plainest teaching of the New Testament.

It may be well, in this connection, to note another feature of Fuller's teaching, which our American Baptists have quite lost sight of. Fuller insisted with all the might he possessed, that faith is the sinner's immediate duty; that there was no duty before "repentance and faith," not even prayer. Nothing is enjoined upon a sinner that does not imply repentance and faith. "It is the duty of ministers not only to exhort their carnal auditors to believe in Jesus Christ for the salvation of their souls, but *it is at our peril to exhort them to anything short of it, or which does not invoice, or imply it.*" The italics here are Mr. Fuller's own, and show the importance he attached to what he was saying. But to shut out all mistake, listen to the following, leveled at some of the preaching of his time: "Repentance towards God, and faith towards our Lord Jesus Christ are allowed to be duties; but not *immediate* duties. The sinner is considered as unable to comply with them, and, therefore, they are not urged upon him; but instead of them he is directed to pray for the Holy Spirit to enable him to repent and believe, and this it seems he can do notwithstanding the aversion of his heart to everything of the kind. But if any man be required to pray for the Holy Spirit, it must be either sincerely, and in the name of Jesus, or insincerely, and in some other way. The latter I suppose will be allowed to be an abomination in the sight of God; he cannot therefore be required to do this; and as to the former, it is just as difficult, and as opposite to the carnal heart as repentance and faith themselves. Indeed, it amounts to the same thing; for a sincere desire after a spiritual blessing, presented in the name of Jesus, is no other than the *prayer of faith.*"

If I knew how to emphasize these words, so that all Baptists in this land would be constrained to take note of them, and prayerfully study them, I would gladly do it. There is just one emphatic point to be made; namely, there is no duty enjoined in the gospel, which does not imply faith and repentance in order to its acceptable performance. It may be doubted if Fuller himself saw the far-reaching significance of his own words, but he did see the simple fact which he states so clearly, otherwise, he could never have put it into phraseology so terse, and so unmistakable as regards, at least, its primary meaning. I cordially commend to all Baptists this significant deliverance of their great leader. And if they shall see, in the light of it, the necessity of changing somewhat their teaching, and reconstructing thoroughly some of their practices, I shall be fully repaid for my labor of love in calling their attention to it.

Meantime, I need only say now, that Fuller and McLean both blundered as to "what is included in believing." Fuller was mistaken as to its including regeneration, or change of heart, *as a prior condition*, and McLean, as to the necessity of excluding from its essence the change of heart, which he admitted to be its immediate effect. Faith, as the ground of justification, is a comprehensive conception. In the last analysis, it is indeed the mind's conviction "of the truth of what God hath said;" the "belief of the gospel;" but not that to the exclusion of any of its divine effects in the soul or in the life. On the contrary, as the principle of justification, it is taken as inclusive of all these effects, and never, for a moment, thought of in the divine mind as apart from them. It is indeed faith which is accounted for righteousness, and not hope, or love, or any other effect of faith, but it is because it is viewed as the root, and ground of all these things, and because they are comprehended in it, as an effect is always included in its cause, that God accepts it for "righteousness," (which, in point of fact, it is not,) and so justifies the obedient believer "freely by his Grace." If a man does not see these things clearly in the dry light of today, it is surely his own fault.

CHAPTER IV:
THE SIMPLE FACTS OF THE CASE

We are now ready to estimate the influence of these various parties upon the mind of Mr. Campbell, and to decide how far the representations of Mr. Whitsitt are entitled to the credence of candid men. It is true that Mr. Campbell read Hervey, Wesley, and Fuller and Gale, Sandeman, McLean, and the Haldanes, and that he was quite familiar with the positions of all these gentlemen, and their arguments in support of them. That their discussions had no influence on the formation of his views, it would be foolish to assert. But, that he followed no one-sided representation is certain, for he carefully read and weighed the arguments of all. If his own statements are entitled to the least credit, he was, more than anything else, a devoted student of the New Testament, and was accustomed to bring all theories and suggestions of theories to the touch-stone of revelation, before receiving or rejecting them. If he was indebted to any one, to Sandeman or McLean, to Wesley or Fuller, for views that he finally held, it was in precisely the same way that every independent and conscientious investigator is indebted to someone else, either directly or indirectly, for the greater part of the truth which he knows. This is as certain as anything human can be. At the same time, it is only fair to say that, in certain of their features, Mr. Campbell's views were kindred to those of McLean and the Haldanes, rather than to those of Fuller and the school of which he was practically the founder. Regarding the *nature* of faith, as then debated, he agreed with Sandeman, McLean and Fuller, as they, confessedly, agreed with each other. Concerning the priority of regeneration or faith, he was with McLean and the Scotch Baptists, and opposed to Fuller and his followers, whether in England or America. He never sympathized with the view that justification by faith implies the exclusion of all the holy dispositions which follow faith, and the imputation of "the bare belief of the bare truth" for righteousness. On this point he was distinctly anti-Sandemanian. His view of the design of baptism was the product of honest and patient study of the New Testament. He borrowed it from no one, nor is it identical with that held by any party since the days of the apostles, and their immediate successors. It is no more the baptismal regeneration of the Greek and Latin fathers, or of Catholics and Anglicans, than it is the notion of a mere outward sign or symbol of an inward grace, now held by Baptists, and, for the most part, Pedo-baptists, alike. It is not baptismal regeneration as it has been held, at any time, by any party. Much less is it the view which represents baptism as a mere symbolical representation of that with which the New Testament has connected it conditionally. To say that he borrowed it from McLean, whose theory required the imputation of faith for righteousness, not only before obedience to any ordinance, but even antecedent to that *holiness of heart* which he robustly held to be an immediate effect of faith, is to talk at random, or to be incapable of making the simplest distinctions of doctrine known to theology. In maintaining the necessity of a plurality of elders, or bishops, in each local church, as well as the observance of the Lord's Supper on every Lord's day, Mr. Campbell agreed substantially with the Sandemanians and Scotch Baptists, because he found them in line with the precedents of the New Testament. Their observance of foot-washing and love-feasts, as ordinances, he rejected, as being destitute of apostolic or inspired support. To this test he brought everything.

That he made no mistakes need not be said, for he was a man, fallible like the rest of us. His greatest admirers have never felt themselves bound to any position he held, unless he was able to show his authority for it in the Word of God. This was his test, and it is theirs likewise. He was no mere theological eclectic, selecting from the great babel about him whatever might happen to strike his own fancy; but a reverent and thoughtful Christian, seeking for the faith and ordinances of the church in the teaching of the inspired apostles of our Lord Jesus Christ. If he felt a certain admiration for the English and Scotch Independents, Baptist or Pedo-baptist, it was mainly because they refused to be bound by human creeds, and bravely asserted their right to the freedom wherewith Christ had made them free. That traces of the influence of Sandeman and the Haldanes may be found in his writings, is unquestionable. There are traces of Alexandrian influence in John's Gospel, as every scholar knows — whether he chooses to say so or not — and yet that fact counts nothing against John's originality as a writer, or the genuineness of the book which bears his name. A work free from any influence from without would be a strange literary product indeed. A theologian whose views should betray no contact with the work of other thinkers, might indeed be considered original, but it is not likely that he would be able to say anything worthy of the world's attention.

In this perfectly legitimate way, and in no other, did Mr. Campbell profit by the labors of other men. The sources of authority which he recognized were in the Scriptures, and he neither received nor rejected anything without reference to scriptural teaching. As regards his real indebtedness to Sandeman and the Scotch Baptist leaders, there has been no pretense of concealment. Prof. Whitsitt naively confesses, even while making a show of original discovery, his dependence upon Mr. C.'s biographer for the facts which explain the coincidences he had otherwise noted. This should have taught him that his imaginary contributions to history are only gleanings from fields which have been duly harvested by others.

Mr. Campbell's absolute independence, as a Biblical student, of all uninspired authority, is nowhere seen more clearly than in the comparison of his views with those of the men from whom it is pretended he borrowed them. He was a Sandemanian, says Prof. Whitsitt; and yet Sandeman was a Calvinist, a Pedo-baptist, and practiced foot-washing, and observed love-feasts while Mr. Campbell was neither a Calvinist nor Pedo-baptist, and held not at all to the Sandemanian customs here mentioned. He had no sympathy with the notion that justification by faith means the imputation of "the bare belief of the bare truth," for righteousness, exclusive of those holy dispositions which are the invariable effects of a sincere belief. On the contrary, he always held that faith justifies and saves, only because it does include — as a cause includes its effects — both change of heart and obedience of life. He never held that faith is purely intellectual, as Prof. W. insinuates. I suspect, if he had undertaken to be closely analytical (a thing he seldom attempted), he would have said that in its ultimate ground, faith is that "act of the mind by which the sinner accepts Jesus as the Christ, the Son of God," or "faith is the belief of the gospel;" or it is the receiving of "the testimony of God concerning his Son." He did say expressly: "Faith is the belief of the gospel." "You can make nothing else out of it, unless you turn it into *confidence*." He might have said, if pressed for strict accuracy, that "confidence is faith by metonomy" but with him faith and confidence were always held to be practically identical, however he might have distinguished between them as a matter of precise definition. He did not share at all, therefore, in that barren intellectualism, which is charged — whether justly or otherwise — against Sandeman. What he really held, was this: faith is the sincere and intelligent belief of the gospel; and such belief always carries in it, by implication, a hearty personal confidence, or trust, in Christ as Redeemer and Savior of men. He never conceived of belief as exclusive of trust, any more than of pious and godly aspirations and volitions as exclusive of belief. If Sandemanianism may be described as "*intellectualism*" Mr. Campbell was no Sandemanian. Faith which did not include in it implicitly both holiness of heart and life, was of no account at all, as he understood the Scriptures. As a matter of fact, from the Baptist point of view, he was more open to the charge of including too much in faith than too little. He never practically separated faith, in justification and salvation, from those godly emotions and activities which are superinduced by means of it. As he looked at the work of redemption, the gospel is the power of God to save only believers, because there is no other way in which gospel power can be conveyed to the hearts and lives of men than by faith. It is not what faith is, as a mere correct verbal definition, that God cares for, but what it means as a source or instrument of divine power in a human soul and life. *It is chiefly the grand possibility of a transformed human life that makes faith valuable in the sight of God.* As Mr. Campbell looked at it, nay, as all the Disciples of Christ see it, if it were not for this wonderful possibility of making sinful men grand and god-like in thought and will and action, we should never have had a word of justification by faith from the lips or pens of inspired men. God counts faith to the believer only for that which he knows is made possible to him by means of it! It is on this principle that faith is "imputed for righteousness," as an act of grace, and through the blood of Christ. And this is the opposite pole of doctrine from that of Sandeman and the Scotch Baptists, as even Prof. Whitsitt would be able to see if he could only get the Baptist film removed from his eyes. No partisan ever sees truth otherwise than from a single angle of vision, and therefore imperfectly.

But, as already stated, Mr. Campbell saw clearly the fact that as regards priority of regeneration (or change of heart) to faith, Andrew Fuller was wrong, while Sandeman and McLean, who placed it among the *effects* of faith, were certainly right. If he really owed this view to those men, his indebtedness was indeed great. It was the most fundamental conception of what may be called his theology. It determined his view of divine influence in conversion and sanctification, as he himself defined those terms, beyond any manner of doubt. Not that it led him to deny the active presence of the Holy Spirit, either in regeneration or in the struggles and conflicts of the Christian life. He made no such denial in either case. What he did do was to explain the influences of the Holy Spirit, as mediated by the Word of God, *i.e.*, as exerted through the Word of God believed. The Scriptures represent the saving power as reaching the heart by faith. But whatever is done before faith, is done without faith, and independently of divine truth, as the means. Nothing could be plainer. Hence, Mr. Campbell did not accept Fuller's doctrine of a change of heart in order to faith. On the contrary, he steadfastly held that all saving power reaches the heart through faith. The ever present Spirit of God moves upon the human soul in, and by, and through, truth believed, and not in a way which dispenses, at any step in the saving process, either with the truth, as it is in Christ, or with the sincere and intelligent belief of it. This is the teaching of the Word of God beyond any sort of doubt. If Sandeman and McLean saw it (which I think they did not, unless very dimly), then the world owes them a great debt, certainly. That Mr. Campbell saw it, admits no denial. And when we shall all see things in the bright light of the Eternal Throne, the fact that he not only saw it, but that he helped the world to see it, and so to disengage itself from many superstitions, will be regarded as one of the mightiest achievements of his long and useful life.

It is perhaps true that Mr. Campbell and the Disciples have made no great original contribution to what is properly known as theology. Our mission under God has not lain in that particular direction. The apostles of Jesus Christ were scarcely theologians in our modern acceptance of the term, though their teaching contains the germs of all the true theology which the world has ever had. They did not trouble themselves over the nice distinctions, which theology seeks, often vainly to settle. They thought in concrete rather than abstract forms. They were concerned not so much about establishing "doctrines," as about saving the souls of men. They were preachers of Christ's gospel to a lost world, not theological professors, working in a realm of abstractions. I do not underestimate the work of the theologian; I magnify that of the preacher. God sends the preacher; the theologian too often sends himself. The gospel was before theology, and it is better than theology. The teacher of "doctrines" may sometimes help us; but oftener, perhaps, he misleads and confuses us. What the sinner needs, above all things, is to have Christ brought intelligently to his heart. The highest knowledge in divine things is to know how to bring saving truth to the understandings and consciences of men. In this direction, mainly, have we found our work. There is no egotism whatever in saying that the popular gospel proclamation has been vastly clarified through our instrumentality. Our influence extends very far outside the bounds of our personal labors, and has reacted upon every orthodox sect in Christendom. This is no idle boast, though men like Mr. Whitsitt may scoff at it. More than any other people known to me, the Baptists have profited by our labors. They may not choose to acknowledge the fact, but it is none the less a fact on that account. The Baptist pulpit is not what it was fifty years ago. It is scarcely necessary to say this to those who are able to recall the days when more than half the Associated Baptists in the West were anti-missionaries, if not thorough antinomians. I know what I am talking about, and the Whitsitts may just as well listen patiently. The change is undeniable. The entire credit of it, of course, is not to be given to the Disciples; neither do they claim it. But Baptist "experiences" are not what they used to be; and for whatever good effects have been wrought at this particular point, they are largely indebted to the Disciples. Certainly we allow somewhat of the change to the general growth of intelligence in their own ministry and people, but even here the Disciples have helped them far more than they are willing to confess.[281]

But to get back to theology. The question whether regeneration — meaning thereby change of heart — is before faith, or through faith, is the chief theological issue we make with the denominations of our time. Other questions are subordinate to this, or are involved in this. The order of the Calvinist is:

(1) Regeneration; (2) Repentance; (3) Faith; (4) Turning to the Lord.

The order of the Armenian is:

(1) Prevenient, or enabling grace; (2) Repentance and seeking the Lord; (3) Faith and regeneration; (4) Turning to the Lord.

The order of the New Testament is:

(1) The intelligent and hearty belief of the gospel; (2) Repentance *upon* (*epi*) the name of Jesus Christ; (3) The actual turning to God; (*i.e.,* in confession of Christ and baptism, and thereafter in obedience to all our Lord's commandments.)

In this last arrangement, repentance is given as equivalent to change of heart, as it is indeed the New Testament designation of it. Such a reconstruction as is here implied, when it has been firmly accomplished in the popular mind, will put the gospel message into harmony with the entire New Testament representation, and also into accord with right reason, as disclosed in the inexorable laws of human thought and experience. A reformation of the Fullerism and Baptist-ism of our time must take place, or its days are as certainly numbered (whether many or few) as truth and rationality are destined to triumph over an obstinate adherence to antiquated errors and superstitions. The question returns therefore:

Is regeneration (change of heart) *before* faith, or *through* faith? Does grace win men to God *through the truth believed*? Or, is "a holy principle

---

[281] [See Henry C. Veddar, *A History of the Baptists in the Middle States*, chapter VII.]

implanted" before faith, and without the instrumentality of the Gospel? What do you say?

Mr. Whitsitt is not the first Baptist scribe who has imagined that he discovered a connection between the views of A. Campbell and those of Sandeman and the Haldanes. If no more than this had been asserted, the matter need have attracted little notice, or none at all. I have already said that traces of such an influence are observable; and I add here, chiefly in the earlier stages of Mr. Campbell's career, though it is not intended to deny that he received some permanent impressions from such sources. The point, however is this: whatever real indebtedness there was in the case, has always been an open fact among the Disciples, and there was never on Mr. Campbell's part, or on theirs, the least effort, or even wish, to conceal it. Mr. Whitsitt has discovered nothing. He has revived a campaign trick which originated in the days of the *Christian Baptist*, and received from Mr. C. himself such attention as he thought it deserved. The only strange thing in the matter is that our doughty professor should have known so little of our history as to imagine that the resemblances in some minor matters which have come to his knowledge in the course of his historical studies, had never attracted the attention of anyone else. In the third volume of the *Christian Baptist*, page 227 (Burnett's edition) may be found a letter to Mr. Campbell from Rev. R.B. Semple, a distinguished Baptist of that day, and immediately following it Mr. Campbell's reply. It suits our purpose here to make some extracts from these rather ancient documents.

Dr. Semple begins with a personal compliment to Mr. Campbell. "Your preaching," he says, "reminds me of Apollos, who displayed, as we moderns say, great talents, or as the Scripture says, was an eloquent man, and mighty in the Scriptures." But even Apollos submitted to be taught in the way of God more perfectly, and so Dr. S. hopes he may be able to do a like service for Mr. Campbell. "So far as I can judge," he continues, "by your writings or preachings, you are substantially a Sandemanian or Haldanian. I know you differ from them in some points, but in substance you occupy their ground. Now I am not about to fall out with them as heretics of the black sort. I think they have many excellent things among them, things I would gladly see more prevalent among us. But in some respects they are far from pure Christianity." He then proceeds to state the counts in his indictment. "Forbearance," he tells us, "is certainly a Christian grace strongly recommended both by precept and example, in the word of God." But in this Christian grace of forbearance, Dr. S. found the Haldanians greatly deficient. He did not regard them as altogether destitute of it, but "they limited its exercise to too narrow bounds." In all church decisions they demanded unanimity; all must think alike. This, Mr. S. regarded as impossible. Men will differ in opinion, and forbearance becomes a necessity. "Among the Haldanians, judging," he says, "from their writings, a gentle spirit is rarely to be found." He considered Mr. Campbell also as conspicuously faulty in this respect. He distinguishes between his writings and his personal bearing in private circles. In such circles he found him, "as a man, mild, pleasant and affectionate;" but his writings "were rigid and satirical beyond all the bounds of Scripture allowance." He regards the *Christian Baptist* as strikingly deficient in a New Testament spirit.

Touching Mr. Campbell's views, he says, "On some other points, I think they are dangerous, unless you are misunderstood; such as casting off the Old Testament, exploding experimental religion in its common acceptation, denying the existence of gifts in the present day, commonly believed to exist among all spiritual Christians, such as preaching, etc. Some other of your opinions, though true, are pushed to extremes, such as those upon the use of creeds, confessions, etc., etc." "In short," he presently adds, "your views are generally so contrary to those of the Baptists in general, that if a party were to go fully into the practice of your principles, I should say a new sect had sprung up, radically different from the Baptists as they now are."

It is not necessary that I should stop to point out the crudeness of Dr. Semple's representation of Mr. Campbell's spirit and aims. It is the fate of every new movement to be misunderstood, and often to be intentionally misrepresented. Of the latter, Dr. S. must be wholly acquitted. Mr. C. always entertained the highest personal regard for him. But he apprehended the new plea imperfectly. This, perhaps, was inevitable, and no one is less disposed than the writer of this review to fight over again the battles of the past, wherever it is clear that they grew out of mere mistakes of the understanding. But touching the question of dependence upon Sandeman and the Haldanes, we shall hear Mr. Campbell himself. I must be allowed to quote at some length:

> You say: "So far as I can judge by your writings and preaching, you are substantially a Sandemanian or Haldanian." This is substantially affirmed of me by many who have never seen nor read one volume of the writings of Sandeman or Haldane; and with the majority it has great weight, who attach to these names something as heretical and damnable as the tenets of Cerinthus and the Nicolaitans. I have not myself ever read all the works of

these men, but I have read more of them than I approve, and more of them than they who impute to me their opinions as heresy.

Concerning Sandeman and Haldane, how they can be associated under one species, is to me a matter of surprise. The former a Pedo-Baptist, the latter a Baptist; the former as keen, as sharp, as censorious, as acrimonious as Juvenal; the latter as mild, as charitable, as condescending as any man this age has produced. As authors I know them well. The one is like a mountain-storm that roars among the cliffs; the other like the balmy zephyrs that breathe upon banks of violets. That their views were the same on some points is as true as that Luther, Calvin and Wesley agreed in many points.

I was once puzzled on the subject of Hervey's dialogues; I mean his Theron and Aspasio. I appropriated one winter season for examining this subject. I assembled all the leading writers of that day on these subjects. I laid before me Robert Sandeman, Hervey, Marshall, Bellamy, Glass, Cudworth, and others of minor fame in this controversy. I not only read, but studied and wrote off in miniature their respective views. I had Paul and Peter, James and John, on the same table; I took nothing upon trust. I do not care for the authority, reputation, or standing of one of the systems, a grain of sand. I never weighed the consequences of embracing any one of the systems as affecting my standing or reputation in the world. Truth — not who says so — was my sole object. I found much entertainment in the investigation. And I will not blush, nor do I fear, to say, that in the controversy, Sandeman was like a giant among dwarfs. He was like Samson with the gates and posts of Gaza upon his shoulders. I was the most prejudiced against him, and the most in favor of Hervey, when I commenced this course of reading. Yet I now believe that not one of them was exactly on the track of the apostles. I have also read Fuller's strictures on Sandemanianism, which I suppose to be the medium of most of the information possessed on that subject in this country. This is the poorest performance Andrew Fuller ever gave the world.

And the fact is (which he indirectly acknowledges) that Andrew Fuller was indebted more to John Glass and Robert Sandeman than to any two men in Britain for the best part of his views. I will not pause to inquire whether he wrote those strictures to save himself from the obloquy of being called a Sandemanian, as some conjecture, or whether he wrote them to give a blow to Archibald McLean of Edinburg, who had driven him from the arena some years before; but I will say it is a very poor production, and proves nothing that either Robert Sandeman or Archibald McLean felt any concern in opposing.

Mr. C. further says, that while he was well acquainted with all this controversy, and while he acknowledged himself debtor to Glass, Sandeman, Hervey, Cudworth, Fuller and McLean, as much as to Luther, Calvin and John Wesley, he candidly and unequivocally avowed that he did not believe any one of them had a clear and consistent view of the Christian religion as a whole.

Still further, he continues:

While I thus acknowledge myself a debtor to those persons, I must say that the debt, in most instances, is a very small one. I am indebted, upon the whole, as much to their errors as to their virtues, for these have been to me as beacons to the mariner, who might otherwise have run upon the rocks and shoals. For the last ten years I have not looked into the works of any of these men, and have lost the taste which I once had for controversial reading of this sort. And during this period my inquiries into the Christian religion have been almost exclusively confined to the Scriptures. I call no man master upon the earth; and although my own father has been a diligent student and teacher of the Christian religion since his youth, and, in my opinion, understands this book as well as any person with whom I am acquainted, yet there is no man with whom I have debated more, and reasoned more than he. I have been so long disciplined in the school of free inquiry, that if I know my own mind, there is not a man upon the earth whose authority can influence me any further than he comes with the authority of evidence, reason and truth.

The ring of these sentences is very clear. There is no affectation, not the least, of concealment. Indebtedness — such as really existed — is frankly acknowledged; yet the narrow limitations of such indebtedness — a fact which is as certain as the other — is distinctly affirmed.

In the *Christian Baptist* (Vol. V. Page 398-400), may be found another letter from Dr. Semple, with another reply from Mr. Campbell. It seems that someone writing in the *Baptist Recorder* over the signature of Querens, desired to see Dr. S. enter the lists as a debater against Mr. Campbell's teaching. To this, the good doctor replied that there was no need of such a discussion. He says: "Mr. Campbell's views are not new, at least not many of them — Sandeman, Glass, the Haldanes were master spirits upon this system many years ago. And they were effectually answered by Fuller and others… If I am called upon, then, to establish my assertions as to Mr. Campbell's views, I refer Querens, and all such, to Fuller's work against Sandeman, &c. I do not know a word in it that I would alter." To this, Mr. Campbell responds as follows:

> *Nor will it do to say that my views, or the cause which I advocate, has been already refuted by any other person. For this will not be satisfactory. To call me a Sandemanian or Haldanian, a Glassite, an Arian, or a Unitarian, and to tell the world that the Sandemanians, Haldanians, etc., etc., have done so and so, and have been refuted by such and such a person, is too cheap a method of maintaining human traditions, and too weak to oppose reason and revelation. You might as well nickname me a Sabellian, an Anthropomorphist, a Gnostic, a Nicolaitan, or an Anabaptist, as to palm upon me any of the above systems. **I do most unequivocally and sincerely renounce each and every one of these systems**. He that imputes any of these systems to me, and ranks me amongst the supporters of them, reproaches me. I do not by this mean to say that there are not in each and all these systems 'many excellent things,' as Bishop Semple himself once said of them…*
>
> *Any one that is well read in these systems, must know that the **Christian Baptist** advocates a cause, and an order of things which not one of them embraced. I repeat; you have only to apply the golden rule to yourself in this instance, and ask yourself how you would like an opponent to call you a Fullerite, a Hopkinsian, an Anabaptist, or something worse, in order to refute your sentiments, when you cordially renounce the systems laid to your charge.*

In the above extract I have emphasized, as the reader will notice, this one sentence: "I do most unequivocally and sincerely renounce each and every one of these systems." That this declaration was not only sincere on Mr. Campbell's part, but that it expressed the simple fact of his relation to these systems, will not be denied by anyone who understands either the systems in question or the aims and principles of Mr. Campbell. And this in spite of any similarity in the use of phrases, such as "the ancient gospel," "the ancient order," etc., or any agreement in certain doctrinal aspects of these systems, which neither Mr. Campbell nor the Disciples have ever denied. The most fundamental conception in our movement, that which gave the mould and form to the whole of it, lies entirely outside, as we shall see presently, of all these systems. But meantime we need to pursue the present phase of our investigation a little further, before dismissing it entirely. Elder William Jones, of London, England, a name not unknown to fame, was a zealous Baptist of the Scotch, or Haldanian school. Between this gentleman and Mr. Campbell there occurred a noteworthy correspondence, parts of which bear immediately upon the subject now before us. Mr. Jones seemed, for a time, to be greatly impressed with Mr. Campbell's work in America, and noticing certain features of it, did not hesitate to identify it, in essentials, with the system which he himself advocated. He speaks of the "Scotch Baptist churches" — addressing Mr. Campbell — "out of which yours in America took their origin, as I think you will not deny." He seems to feel that Mr. C. was scarcely willing to do justice to these Scotch Baptists, or to acknowledge the real extent of his indebtedness to them. He more than intimates the existence of some sort of vainglory, in the desire to appear more original than he really was. This desire, he thought, had led him to undervalue the work of Archibald McLean and his coadjutors, Braidwood, Ingles, Peddie, etc., etc., in the Scotch Baptist connection. In this vein he wrote a long letter, which will be found in the *Millennial Harbinger* for 1835, page 295. I need make no extracts from this letter. It is a spirited vindication of the Scotch Baptists, but betrays an utter inability to distinguish between them and the movement Mr. Campbell was leading in America. This, perhaps, should not be thought strange, since mere incidental resemblances in detail are often mistaken by thoughtless persons for identity in essential principles. Besides, Elder Jones' acquaintance with Mr. Campbell's writings was at this time very imperfect, and he was not nearly so anxious to claim kinship with him when he discovered a disposition on Mr. C.'s part to treat somewhat irreverently the strict Calvinism of the communities whose cause he plead so earnestly. True, he repudiates "hyper-Calvinism," and says, "My recollection does not at this moment furnish me with the names of three individuals who are tinctured" with it. But, at the same time, Mr. Jones, if not a "hyper-Calvinist," was really a Calvinist of a very "strait" fashion, as the event clearly showed. This, however, would have made no difference with Mr. Campbell, as regards the matter of fellowship. The difference in this case came from the other side. And this single fact discloses, partially at least, the wide difference between the two systems. But I wish to quote briefly from Mr. Campbell's reply to Elder Jones' letter. I begin near the close of the 103rd page:

> *How much the reformation for which we plead is indebted to the labors of those revered fathers of the Scotch Baptist churches, I am not able to say. For my own part. I am greatly indebted to all the reformers, from Martin Luther down to John Wesley. I could not enumerate or particularize the individuals, living and dead, who have assisted in forming my mind. I am in some way indebted to some person or other for every idea I have on every subject. Bilworth and McCrae, with their spelling- books — Euclid, Locke, Bacon and Newton, and ten thousand others, cast an eye upon me... How many have, in the way of moral causation, excited my mind to this train of reasoning, or to the examination of this fact or that incident, I am now, and will be while life lasts, wholly unable to say.*

> *I may therefore be indirectly indebted to Archibald McLean, for example, more than I am aware. A few years after my immersion, I read one volume of his tracts, and I don't know that I have ever read but his review of Wardlaw's Lectures, his Reply to Fuller, a Defense of Believer's Baptism, The Substance of two Discourses on Faith, preached at Kingston-on-Hull, and a treatise on the Commission.*

> *But while on this subject of originality, and the acknowledgment of literary and moral debts of thought, I soon found that our worthy friend McLean and the Edinburg school had drawn largely and liberally from the writings and labors of Robert Ferrier, Jas. Smith, John Glass, etc., that school which began its operations in 1728, about 40 years before the date of the Scotch Baptist churches.*

> *This egotistic narrative is due to my Scotch and English brethren. I would have them know that we are in possession of all their knowledge, and thankfully acknowledge our debts to the great and wise and good men who have gone before us. I thank my Heavenly Father that I was born at the proper time, and on the best spot on the earth, and surrounded with the best set of circumstances to afford me the best religious education which the 19th century could furnish.*

And yet after all these acknowledgments, Mr. C. goes on to insist that he had "views of the Christian Institution *wholly new* as far as the works of all the schools to which he had alluded were concerned." It is scarcely worthwhile to say that these things wholly new, as regards these schools, were considered by Mr. C., and are now considered by all the Disciples, as the most fundamental and far-reaching features of his attempt to restore the apostolic gospel and institutions to the world. Nor can any well-informed man question this fact, unless his prejudices have gotten the better of his judgment. The resemblance to the Scotch Baptists is merely a coincidence in certain features, while the informing principle, the molding and fashioning idea of the later movement is altogether different. We do not care to insist upon this fact, except to vindicate the truth of history and give honor to whom honor is due. We would just as soon trace our origin to the Scotch Baptists, or the Sandemanians, as to any other human source, if such were the case. Why should we care? The only question we ask is, *What is truth? What is from God?* We are concerned not a farthing as to who said a thing, or who before us has taught as we teach, till we get back to Christ and his apostles. The authority of Alexander Campbell sits as lightly upon our consciences as that of Fuller, or Gill, or Sandeman, when we find him contending against right reason, or the word of God. "Sworn to no master, of no sect am I," is true of every man who clearly understands himself, as a Disciple of Jesus Christ. Nothing is truth to him, till he finds it in the oracles of God, so far as his religion is concerned. He may respect and love the great and good men who have gone before him, *but he believes in Jesus only.*

It is due to the memory of Mr. Campbell, that his personal testimony, concerning the matters treated of in this chapter, should be fairly and fully stated. It so happens that there is no lack of material for this purpose. In the Millennial Harbinger for 1848, will be found a series of articles devoted to these very questions. The first number of this series begins on page 279. I quote the following from page 280:

> *The question has often been propounded to me — how came you by your present views of the Christian religion? Are they original or derived? If original, by what process of reason? If derived, from what authority or source? These are questions of but little consequence to any individual. The capital question is: **are they well founded?***

To this, Mr. C. presently adds: "There are no new discoveries in Christianity. *Our whole religion, objectively and doctrinally considered, is found in a book.* Whatever in Christianity is new, is not true. Whatever is true, is contained in the commonly received and acknowledged books of the Old and New Testaments, or Covenants." The whole question, he urges, "is one of interpretation." It has respect to what is written in these books. But still the question recurs:

> *How were you led to interpret the Scriptures differently, and to teach and practice differently from what you once thought, and believed and practiced? Well, as these may be useful to others, I will answer the question by the narration of a few incidents, anecdotes and facts, some of which, never before published, may be of use to others, and lead them to a new mode of thinking and acting, as well as of enjoying the Christian religion.*

It will be seen that the very question which furnishes the thesis for Prof. Whitsitt's book, is that which Mr. Campbell here sets himself to answer. He begins, of course, with what he regards as the essential starting point of his investigations, the point of his departure from the views in which he had been trained by his honored father, and the church of which he had been a member from his infancy. He does not deny his intellectual indebtedness to anyone, orthodox or heterodox, Catholic or Protestant. His task is to give faithfully the lines along which his mind, as he devoutly believed, had been providentially led from first to last. This would answer the question which men were asking him; the very question, as I have said, which Mr. Whitsitt attempts to answer in his pretentious little book. Where, then, does he place the initial movement of this whole process of study and development, which issued in the formation of the views, to the advocacy of which he gave the maturest and most fruitful years of his life? If a man wished to know the real answer to Prof. Whitsitt's question, here is the place to obtain it. All the essential facts are here given in a most straightforward and lucid way. There can be no excuse for ignorance in the matter at all. It is not said that no impression had been made upon his mind by Greville Ewing, or John Walker, or anyone else, but as the real point of departure, as the initial impulse of all that he himself regarded as most characteristic in his conception of the Christian religion, he refers us to certain words which deeply impressed him, and set his mind to work in an entirely new direction. I still quote from the *Harbinger*, as above, page 280:

> *The first proof-sheet that I ever read was a form of my father's* **Declaration and Address** *in press in Washington, Pennsylvania, on my arrival there in October, 1809. There were in it the following sentences:* "**Nothing ought to be received into the faith or worship of the church, or be made a term of communion**

> *amongst Christians, that is not as old as the New Testament. Nor ought anything to be admitted as of divine obligation, in the church constitution and management, but what is expressly enjoined by the authority of our Lord Jesus Christ and his apostles upon the New Testament church;* **either in express terms or by approved precedent.** *"*

These words, be it noted, relate to the *constitution* of the church of Christ, to its principle of affiliation and bond of brotherhood. If they mean anything — and the man is queerly constituted who does not perceive their far-reaching import — they relate to what is fundamental in the church as a divine institution, and are, therefore, of the highest importance. These last words, Mr. Campbell says, "made a deep impression" on his mind. The attempt of Whitsitt to connect Alexander Campbell with the preparation of this address is entirely gratuitous, not to say impertinent. It is puerile if gravely held; as the device of an advocate, it is scarcely less than contemptible. Mr. Campbell speaks of these words as the words of his father. He expressly says, *"They made a deep impression on my mind."* You must discredit utterly his own testimony before you can believe that he had anything to do with the putting of these words into the address. Mr. C. says there was "ambiguity about the 'approved precedent,' but none about 'express terms.'" These words became a study to him. He "reasoned with himself and others" on the matters involved in them. Like any man who sees for the first time the force of a great and fruitful generalization, his whole intellectual nature was quickened and aroused. He "reasoned with himself and with others." This expression well indicates his absorption with the theme, and shows at the same time its causal relation to the whole development which followed.

While these studies, these "reasonings with himself and others," were going on, he met with Rev. Mr. Riddle of the Presbyterian church, and introduced the matter to him. But Mr. Riddle, admitting the words in question to be plausible, pronounced them unsound. "If you follow them out," said he, "you must become a Baptist." This was well said. But there was more in these words than mere Baptistism, as distinguished from Presbyterianism. And it was this excess of meaning beyond the baptismal question which was the secret of their absorbing interest to Mr. C., for it appears that he had not yet weighed their bearing on that particular controversy. His father, who had written the address, had not suspected the conclusion wrapped up in his own formula. Like many another man, he was providentially "building wiser than he knew," as the sequel clearly proved.

"What," said Mr. C., in response to Mr. Riddle, "is there no express precept for, nor precedent of, infant baptism in the Scriptures?"

Doctor Riddle said, "Not one."

Mr. Campbell says, "I was startled."

Turning to Mr. Andrew Monroe, the principal bookseller of Jefferson College, Cannonsburg, Pa., Campbell said, "send me, if you please, forthwith, all the treatises you have in favor of infant baptism." The treatises were sent. And here began, unexpectedly, as the circumstances show, the studies which ended in the immersion of the Campbells, and the formation of the church at Brush Bun, Pennsylvania, on the foundation divinely ordained by our Lord Jesus Christ. The account of this matter given in Prof. Whitsitt's book, (chapter 8) is a miserable perversion of the facts. A careful manipulation of extracts from Dr. Richardson's Life of Campbell, skillfully interwoven with suggestive inventions from his own brain, imparts an appearance of plausibility to a story which wrongs the Campbells, and leaves our author without the slightest claim to the character of an impartial historian. It is a conspicuous example of what is, alas, too common — viz: perversion of history to serve the purpose of a party. Fair-minded Baptists have affirmed as much, and it is greatly to their credit that they have done so.[282]

Mr. Campbell says he never inquired for anything on the Baptist side. He was impressed with the idea that they were an ignorant people, and had no thought of deriving assistance from such a source. He had read John Bunyan's *Pilgrim's Progress*, but knew not that he was a Baptist. It is not strange that Mr. C. should have had such an impression regarding the Baptists of that day. It is doubtful whether one young man in a hundred of Presbyterian raising had a different view. Besides, the Baptists were not then the educated people they are now. They had had men of distinction among themselves, but even their ablest men had won little recognition among the Pedo-Baptist sects. All the members of "the Washington Christian Association" were Presbyterians, and hostile to Baptist views. Mr. C. says expressly that he "was better pleased with Presbyterianism than anything else, and desired, if possible, to maintain it." (*Harbinger*, p. 281).

His study of the books sent him did not impress him at all favorably. Indignant at their "assumptions and fallacious reasonings," he threw them aside in disgust, and hurried to his Greek New Testament with a

---

[282] See Appendix.

hope of finding something more satisfactory. But here he found no resting-place for the sole of his foot. He went to his father for help. It was a question of "precept and precedent," of course. It was from this point of view his inquiries had begun, and his investigations had undoubtedly taken that direction throughout. His father conceded the whole ground as to the precept or precedent for infant baptism, but, "strange to tell," says the son, "took the ground that once in the church, and participants of the Lord's Supper, we could not 'unchurch or paganize ourselves' — and commence again as would a heathen man and a publican." (p. 281).

They went into discussion. The father admitted that they ought not to teach or practice infant baptism without divine authority, that they ought to practice only the apostolic baptism, but insisted that they ought not to unchristianize themselves after having professed and preached the Christian faith, and participated in its most solemn ordinances. This and kindred questions were discussed for "many months." Finally the end came. Alexander told his father — he says "with great reluctance" — that he dissented from all his reasonings upon the subject, and that he must be baptized. He was now fully satisfied, as he expressly tells us, that he had never been baptized, and to have hesitated would have been to be untrue to his deliberate convictions. It was doubtless a great struggle, but Alexander Campbell was not the sort of a man that hesitates long, when Scripture and conscience demand a forward movement, at whatever cost of cherished memories and affections. What his father might do, what other dear friends might do, he knew not. The decision made was by himself, and for himself alone. The baptism accordingly took place, but greatly to his gratification, his father and sister, his wife, and several others went with him.

He had stipulated with Elder Luce, the administrator, that he should be baptized upon the New Testament confession of Jesus as the Christ, the Son of God. Perhaps Prof. Whitsitt would regard this scrupulous adherence to the scriptural formula of profession as a specimen of Sandemanian "literalism," but he does not intimate that it was a slavish following of Sandemanian precedent. He says indeed that it was stipulated that the baptism "should be performed *into the name* of the Father, etc., and not *in the name*, as was then, and now is usual among the Regular Baptists. "This," he tells us, was "in due subjection to the authority of Archibald McLean." Does Prof. Whitsitt intend to be understood as taking position against this rendering of the commission? Of course he does not. What then can save his statement from classification with the characteristic devices of all demagogues? Verily, the wily and unscrupulous leaders of our partisan politics are not the only demagogues in the world.

The baptism of the Campbells took place on the 12th day of June, 1812. In his usual sneering manner, Mr. Whitsitt says that "during the period between the year 1812 and 1820, Alexander relapsed into a condition of mere vegetation." Vegetation, forsooth! There is every reason to believe that this was one of the most important periods of his life, the period pre-eminently in which the great germinal principles that shaped the thought and work of his whole life were becoming distinctly formed in his mind. Concerning this very period, Mr. C. writes — *Harbinger* 1848, p. 344 —

> *The position of baptism itself to the other institutions of Christ became a new subject of examination, and a very absorbing one. A change of any one's views in any radical matter in all its practical bearings and effects upon all his views, not only in reference to that simple result, but also in reference to all its connections with the whole system of which it is a part, is not to be computed a priori, by himself or anyone else.*

The change of his views on baptism, according to Mr. C. himself, was the beginning of a most careful study of the whole Christian religion from the standpoint of the advance already made.

> *I must know now two things about everything — its **cause** and its **relations**. Hence my mind was for a time set loose from all its moorings. It was not a simple change of views on baptism, which happen a thousand times without anything more, but a **new commencement**. I was placed on a new eminence — a new peak of the mountain of God, from which the whole landscape of Christianity presented itself to my mind in a new attitude and position.*

"Mere vegetation," indeed! Did Paul "relapse into a condition of mere vegetation" during that mysterious sojourn in Arabia after his conversion? Perhaps Prof. Whitsitt thinks so; and if he were writing a caricature of the apostle's life, instead of Alexander Campbell's, it would be exactly like him to say so. Paul has nowhere given in detail the processes of elaboration and adjustment through which his mind had struggled into the full light of the gospel, but that he had such an experience of the gradual opening up of the truth to his soul cannot be doubted. A great intellect like Paul's must have time to take its bearings, and shape the outline of its activities in the new field of sacrifice and toil, which now lay before him. Paul did not "vegetate;" nor did Alexander Campbell. Neither of them was that sort of man.

Prof. Whitsitt speaks very slightingly of Mr. Campbell's sermon on The Law, delivered in 1816, in the very midst of the period designated as one of "mere vegetation" — doubtless because there is nothing in it (although he more than insinuates the contrary) which tends to strengthen the thesis which he has undertaken to prove. If he had really wished to follow Mr. Campbell along the lines of his actual growth in divine knowledge, he would not have passed over this memorable discourse so lightly. The fact is, that more than anything else in our possession, this sermon indicates the true nature of the revolution which was going on in his mind. The germs indeed of very much of the most characteristic teaching of his life are contained in it. The clear, comprehensive, and fruitful distinction between the old and new Covenants, between Christianity and Judaism, between the law and the gospel, which did so much to shape the whole movement of the Disciples, is here fully propounded and convincingly argued. And so far away is the general tenor of the discourse from the fixed grooves of Sandemanian theology, that so distinguished a leader of the Scotch Baptists as Elder William Jones of London — a Sandemanian, as Prof. Whitsitt would say, of the Immersion observance — boldly rejected it as downright Antinomianism. Criticizing an article in the *Christian Baptist* of exactly the same purport, he says:

> *Here is a strange affair indeed; Mr. Campbell, who exhibits the Scotch Baptists* [Sandemanians, according to Prof. Whitsitt, of the immersion observance] *of this country as being fettered and manacled and paralyzed by the stays of "Hyper-Calvinism," is himself found chiming in with the Hyper-Calvinists, the only party on this side the Atlantic that has the least hesitation in admitting the perpetual obligation of the Decalogue, and on a point too in which the Scotch Baptist churches are firmly agreed in opposing both. **On this point you are quite out of our camp, and we find you in that of our enemies** — Millennial Harbinger,* 1835. Page 540.

This extract, as I have said, is part of Elder Jones' comment upon an article to the same effect as the Sermon on The Law to which our Professor refers in a semi-contemptuous vein. But as a matter of fact this sermon demonstrates that Mr. Campbell's mind was not only moving in directions wholly unsuggested by those teachers whom Prof. Whitsitt represents him as slavishly following, but oftentimes reaching conclusions utterly opposed to their most fundamental ideas. This will not be questioned, I believe, by any candid person acquainted with all the facts. That my readers may see clearly what fruitful germs are contained in this sermon, I give the following extracts:

> *Now, is it not most obvious that this text [Gal. 3:24] and context, instead of countenancing law-preaching, condemn it? The scope of it is to show that whatever use the law served as a schoolmaster previous to Christ, it no longer serves that use. And now that Christ has come, we are no longer under it… Some, not withstanding the plainness of this doctrine, may urge their own experience as contrary to it. It would, however, be as safe for Christians to make divine truth a test of their experience, and not their experience a test of divine truth. Some individuals have been awakened by the appearance of the Aurora Borealis, by an earthquake, by a thunderstorm, by a dream, by sickness, etc. How inconsistent for one of these to affirm from his own experience that others must be awakened in the same way! How incompatible with truth for others to preach such occurrences as preliminary to saving conversion!*
>
> *A fourth conclusion which is deducible from the above premises is, that all arguments and motives, drawn from the law, or Old Testament, to urge the disciples of Christ to baptize their infants; to pay tithes to their teachers; to observe holy days or religious fasts, as preparatory to the observance of the Lord's supper; to sanctify the seventh day; to enter into national covenants; to establish any form of religion by civil law; — and all reasons and motives borrowed from the Jewish law to excite the disciples of Christ to a compliance with, or imitation of, Jewish customs, are inconclusive, repugnant to Christianity, and fall ineffectual to the ground; **not being enjoined or countenanced by the Lord Jesus Christ**.*

This last sentence is the key-note to the entire sermon. The authority of Moses has been superseded. Everything stands or falls accordingly as it is supported or unsupported by Christ's authority. Nothing is binding now because Moses commanded it. Only the things of Moses which have been "repromulged" by Jesus Christ are binding on his disciples. Prof. Whitsitt may not think very highly of the doctrine of this sermon, but he can find no vestige of Sandemanianism in it. For all that, however, it follows very closely, if not "slavishly," one of Mr. Campbell's great leaders — the apostle to the Gentiles.

The year 1820, which is fixed by our Professor as the later limit of this assumed vegetation period, brings us to the debate with Mr. Walker, the Presbyterian, and to the beginning of Mr. Campbell's career as an author. The McCalla debate and the *Christian Baptist* came in 1823, and from that time on his whole public life was before the eyes of the world. Much that he wrote in the earlier years of his editorial activity must be taken as tentative rather than final. His mind was in the growing stage even yet, and the conclusions then reached often failed, no doubt, to command the assent of his judgment at a later period. It is always so in great mental revolutions. And the religious reformer must therefore be studied in the light of this inexorable law which shapes our progress in every sort of knowledge. To its operation there has been thus far no exception in human history.

CHAPTER V:
A MOST FUNDAMENTAL DIFFERENCE

Compared with the varieties of the Scottish Independent, whether Baptist or Pedo-Baptist, the history of the Disciples exhibits from the commencement a most striking difference. From the first step taken, the Campbells looked to the union of Christians as one special object of their labors. If they rejected human creeds, it was because they were essentially schismatic in their tendencies. If they repudiated the jargon of scholasticism, it was that hindrances to Christian unity might be gotten out of the way. If they emphasized the simple features of the apostolic gospel, and church order, it was because they were firmly persuaded that the catholicity of our Lord's prayer (John 17) could never be attained upon any complex doctrinal basis of human contrivance. If they would have no term of fellowship not enjoined by our Lord Jesus Christ, either in express precept, or by good, sound precedent, the reason was still the same. The restoration of the New Testament faith and polity was no doubt a thing to be sought on its own account, but the necessity of seeking it first became clear to them, when engaged in studying the conditions of spiritual and ecclesiastical fellowship.

Abraham Lincoln once said, in substance: "My business is to preserve the Union. Whatever I do has reference to this one thing especially. If I set the slaves free, it will be to save the Union; if I can save the Union better without setting them free, then I shall not set them free. The one thing to be done is to save the Union." It was very much so with the Campbells. They had seen the evil of division. Sectism was to them a sin of no common magnitude. From this great sin they felt that our common Protestantism should be saved. It was at this point our movement began, and this end has never been lost sight of for a moment, in our whole history. It is impossible now that we should lose sight of it at any future period. We must ever pray in the words of our Lord; "that they may all be one, as the Father and the Son are one, to the end that the world may believe." We have always emphasized the importance of unity as no other Protestant community has done. And today, when it is fashionable to plead that Evangelical Protestantism has all the unity the Lord ever contemplated, our voice is still heard above the din and clamor of sects pleading in the Master's name for a union of disciples of which the only adequate measure is the oneness of God and his Son, Jesus Christ; a union which shall be outward and actual, so that the world may be constrained to believe in God's love, manifest through his Son, to our whole sinning and dying race. To urge this plea for Christian unity, as no other people is urging it, is one of the reasons of our existence; one of the reasons which shall justify our presence among the active forces of Christendom, in the day when God shall judge the world. Of this, we can no more doubt, than we can call in question the words of the Master upon which our faith is built.

The whole Scotch school of Independents, whether headed by Glass and Sandeman, or McLean and the Haldanes, overlooked this great question almost entirely. They sought *doctrinal* truth, as the one paramount object of all their investigations and discussions. I do not say that they lost sight of everything else absolutely, but I do say that their chief distinction was doctrinal and speculative. Of the scriptural basis of ecclesiastical fellowship and cooperation, they seem to have had no clear conception at all. To differ doctrinally on some hair-splitting abstraction, was to insure division and the formation of a new party. The sect-making tendency, which has been the bane of Protestantism from the days of Luther and Calvin, was pre-eminently the bane of Scotch Independency. They were born separatists, one and all. In the light of eternity, this will be the chief thing to be said against them. The Sandemanian errors regarding faith, for which they have had many hard things written about them in our time, will then appear to be venial[283] blunders, compared with this more serious mistake. *Separation, without a justifying necessity in the sight of God, is a great sin.*

From the inception of their work, the Campbells seem to have caught the true scriptural idea of ecclesiastical fellowship. They soon learned to distinguish broadly between the faith which saves men, and doctrinal beliefs which neither save nor condemn them. Between the belief with the heart that Jesus is the Christ, God's only begotten Son, and all the theological opinions which make up our various Protestant orthodoxies, they drew a broad, bold line, and made it ever thereafter ineffaceable. The faith that saves the soul, they said, is the faith which unites to God, and which should unite God's children to one another. The faith which God accepts, his church should accept also. If God cares not for our theological abstractions, however necessary they may seem to the symmetry of the doctrine of redemption, then we should not care for them. It is a sin to require men to agree with us in matters wherein God does not require agreement with him. With this clear-cut, comprehen-

---

[283] [Mild, forgivable.]

sive, divine deliverance, the Campbells began. They saw many things, no doubt, as in a mirror, very obscurely, but this they saw with a clearness and distinctness, which, under the circumstances, was absolutely marvelous. No doubt others had denounced human creeds before they denounced them, and had talked about the Bible, as a sufficient rule in all matters of faith and life, before they began their distinctive work as reformers. But the Campbells saw a reason for the repudiation of creeds which others had not seen. They perceived clearly that when used as bonds of fellowship, they rendered the unity of the church an absolute impossibility. There is not a denominational creed in Christendom that does not contain in it dogmatic utterances which lie outside the limits of the common faith — the faith which a man must have, or it is written against him: "He that believeth not shall be condemned." This common faith which all Christians have — which a man must have before he can become a Christian — was the faith-basis of the whole church of God in the New Testament times. In those days, the one common formula of Christian profession was that which had been divinely ordained — "I believe that Jesus is the Christ, the Son of God." Arianism and Athanasianism were yet unknown. Augustinianism and Pelagianism had not been heard of. Calvinism and Arminianism lay concealed in the womb of the far-away centuries.

Mind, we do not object to the formulation of individual beliefs. And if a company of Christian believers should wish to give expression to their theological ideas for general information, we do not say there would be any harm in it. From the days of the Campbells the distinction between such expressions of opinion and the creed-made tests of ecclesiastical fellowship in use throughout our modern Christendom, has been clearly and distinctly drawn. The publication of my individual opinions, simply as my opinions, can harm no one, but the dogmatic proclamation of such opinions as a basis of fellowship and church cooperation, is an impertinence in the eyes of God and all thoroughly instructed Christian men. The difference here is open and palpable, and any pretended failure to see it is without excuse. A theological development, more or less elaborate, from the great germinal ideas of the New Testament was to be expected — was, indeed, according to the fixed laws of human thought, inevitable. It is not against theology, as such, that our movement is a protest. Theology in itself is well enough. Of course, where there are contradictions in theology there must be error, as well as truth. But all theology is not error. Our point is this: The unity of believers in one spiritual organism or fellowship was, beyond doubt or denial, the archetypal conception of the church in the mind of the Redeemer. No man uncommitted to the advocacy of a sect, it is perfectly safe to say, can object to this statement.

But is this divine ideal of the dear Lord a practical one? Or is it purely visionary, never to be realized in the church's history? Everything depends on the answer to this question. Mind, I do not ask whether, under the ordinary laws of human thought and association, it has been a practical ideal in the times which are gone, but is it an ideal that we may expect to see historically realized under God's gracious administration at any time this side the judgment day? Our movement implies the possibility, under God, of a united church. Nay, more; it implies the hope, the confident persuasion, grounded in Scripture, that the prayer of the Lord Jesus will be realized before the church's mission is accomplished; before the world shall have been converted to Christ. The Papacy maintains, after a sort, an outward unity which the whole world recognizes. But the Papacy is a spiritual despotism. The individual is lost in the collective organization. The Hierarchy controls everything. Free, honest investigation for truth's sake, for salvation's sake even, is not to be thought of. The church — that is, the priesthood — does all the thinking which is needed. The individual, even though he be a priest, is mentally a serf. But Protestantism affirms man's spiritual birthright, in Christ. It sets before us an open Bible, and bids us seek truth for ourselves. This is its crown of glory for all the ages. But is division the price of this freedom? Is our modern denominationalism the best that is possible on the Protestant principle of the right of private judgment? If such be the case, I do not say we are purchasing our spiritual enfranchisement at too great a cost — for what equivalent is there for the soul's freedom — but this I say, I do not believe that such is the fact in the case. It is impossible that such can be the case. If Protestantism, in its fundamental idea, be of God, then it does not make our Lord's intercessory prayer an impossibility.

But where then is the seat of the trouble, whose existence it were madness to deny? I answer: In the mistake made by the sixteenth century reformers touching the law of affiliation, or bond of fellowship, in the church of God. The New Testament faith-basis has been rejected, and in its place has been substituted, everywhere, a body more or less complete, of theological opinion. Every Protestant denomination on earth is an example of such rejection and substitution. The theological articles of faith — so called — differentiate the parties, and measure the extent of theological divergence between them. But is there not, it may be asked, beneath all this diversity of the evangelical denominations, a deeper and most real unity? The unity for which the Lord prayed? To the first question we answer, yes. To the second question, no. There is a real, vital union, certainly, between all Christians, but any union which is not actual, historical, and therefore outward, is not an adequate fulfillment of the Lord's prayer. Remember, Jesus says, "I pray that they may all be one, as we are one, that the world may believe that thou hast sent me." Now, sect-strife, more than anything else, hinders the world's conversion to Christ. It is so here at home. It is doubly so in heathen lands abroad. This question is coming home to us more and more. We must face it, whether we wish to do so or not. What our missionaries among the heathen are learning today, the Lord Jesus saw, through the vistas of twenty centuries, from the very beginning. No; the Lord's people are not one in the sense of his prayer. This is absolutely certain. They will never be one in that sense until "the rock" upon which he built his church is restored to its proper place. But this is objected to. Our Lord's idea, we are told, was that of unity in diversity. Now it must be admitted that "unity in diversity" is a happy phrase, and that it may be used to express a great truth. Only let us beware that we do not employ it to conceal a great falsehood! It must be plain to every man of sense, that no unity of Christians other than one which is consistent with a certain sort of diversity is at all possible. In theological tenets, Christian men need never expect absolute agreement. It was not so in the beginning, and it is safe to say it never will be. But in faith, saving faith, by universal consent, Christians are, and must ever be, one. Nothing is plainer, therefore, than the fact, that so far as faith is concerned, here is a sufficient basis for a unity both spiritual and ecclesiastical. It will be sufficient, if we require, as a condition of fellowship with us, precisely the same *faith* which God requires as a condition of fellowship with him. Nay, more; is it not at our peril that we require anything else? I judge no one; but certainly there is a day of reckoning to come. Judgment is to begin at the house of God.

Now, of these things, the Campbells seem to have had an unusually clear understanding from a very early period in their work. Something like this discloses itself in the first tentative beginnings in the "Christian Association." It grows clearer at each successive step. Along this line God was leading them. Slowly the wide field is opened up before them, and the progress, upon the whole, is steady in the direction of the first forward outlook. The final expression of this great feature in our history is, perhaps, nowhere better put than by Mr. Campbell in his debate with Dr. N.L. Rice, at Lexington, Ky.:

So is it in our most holy faith. There are but two grand prin-

*ciples in Christianity, two laws revealed and developed, whose combination produces similar harmony, beauty, and loveliness in the world of mind as in the world of matter. I must at once declare the simplicity of this divine constitution of remedial mercy. It has but three grand ideas peculiar to itself; and these all concern the King. I am sorry that this mysterious and sublime simplicity does not appear to those who set about making constitutions for Christ's kingdom. This confession of omnipotent moral power, because the offspring of infinite wisdom and benevolence, must be learned from one passage, Matt. 16, "Who do men say that I am?" We must advance one step further — who say **you** that I am? Peter in one momentous period expressed the whole affair — "**Thou art the Christ, the Son of the living God.**" The two ideas expressed, concern the **person** of the Messiah and his **office.** The one implied concerns his **character;** for it was through his character, as developed, that Peter recognized his person and his Messiahship. Now, let us take the shoes from off our feet, for we stand on holy ground. "Blessed art thou, Simon, son of Jonas; flesh and blood hath not revealed it unto thee, but my Father, who is in heaven. And I say unto thee, thou art Peter (a stone) and on **this rock** I will build **my church,** and the gates of hell (hades) shall not prevail against it." It will stand forever. "I will give unto thee (thyself alone, Peter,) the keys of the kingdom of heaven (my church), and whatsoever thou shalt bind on earth, shall be bound in heaven; and whatsoever thou shalt loose on earth, shall be loosed in heaven." Here, then, is the whole revelation of the mystery of the Christian constitution. The full confession of the Christian faith. All that is peculiar to Christianity is found in these words; not merely in embryo, but in a clearly expressed outline. A clear perception, and a cordial belief of these two facts will make any man a Christian. He may carry them out in their vast dimensions and glorious developments, to all eternity. He may ponder upon them until his spirit is transformed into the image of God; until he shines in more than angelic brightness, in all the purity and beauty of heavenly love. Man glorified in heaven, gifted with immortality, and rapt in the ecstasies of eternal blessedness, is but the mere result of a proper apprehension of, and conformity to, this confession. I am always overwhelmed with astonishment in observing how this document has been disparaged and set at naught by our builders of churches. Yet Jesus calls it the rock. It is in a figure of a church or* *a temple, the foundation, the rock. When all societies build on this one foundation, and on it only, then there shall be unity of faith, of affection, and of cooperation; but never till then. Every other foundation is sand. Hence they have all wasted away. Innumerable parties have perished from the earth; and so will all the present, built on any other foundation than this rock... Their doom is written, "Dust thou art, and unto dust shalt thou return." (Campbell and Rice Debate, page 422).*

From this masterly statement I would gladly quote more; but space forbids. Whoever confesses Jesus, as above described, receiving him in his heart as Messiah and Savior, and then, because he has so received him, is baptized into the name of the Father, Son, and Holy Spirit, becomes thereby a member of the church of God, and is so owned and approved in heaven; not only so, is thereby entitled to be so owned and approved in every congregation or local church of God on earth. This is the beginning. A life so begun, and continued in faithful conformity to Christ's life till the end comes, is sure to be approved of God in the judgment. This faith and life constitute the New Testament law of affiliation, the one divine bond of Christian and church fellowship, ordained by Jesus Christ, till he comes to judge the world. Of some things a man may not feel sure. Of this we are as sure as we are that the only name in which men can be saved is the name of Jesus. Every deviation from this law of divine brotherhood and cooperation is outside the divine charter, and is doomed to failure in the future, as it has failed in the past. This the Campbells clearly saw, and this the Sandemanians and Scotch Baptists, like all other parties, utterly failed to see. If there were nothing else to be said to their honor, there is enough in this single restoration of the primitive ideal to insure to them the reverent regard of true men in all the ages to come.

CHAPTER VI:
CERTAIN MATTERS OF DETAIL

Prof. Whitsitt, without a word of authority from any source, seeks to make the impression that the course of Thomas Campbell in America, was really inspired by Alexander, while he was yet in Glasgow, Scotland. I call attention to the following extract, as a specimen:

> *From the letter of protest that was addressed by Mr. Campbell to that body [the Associate Synod of North America], it may be gathered that the objections urged against him related to the usual Sandemanian scruples concerning the impropriety of any human standards of belief, and to his advocacy of the customary Sandemanian position that the Scriptures are the only admissible standard, to the exclusion of all kinds of creeds and confessions of faith. Here was the earliest, if not the most brilliant, conquest which Alexander was enabled to make on behalf of Sandemanianism.*

This intimation of an influence exerted, first upon Alexander Campbell by Greville Ewing, and then upon Thomas Campbell through his son, need not be noticed here, further than to say that there is no shadow of foundation for it anywhere outside Prof. W.'s own imagination. Not only is it without authority, the facts are against it. The younger Campbell was in Glasgow, busily pursuing his studies in the University, being at the same time charged with the care of his father's family. How should he find time to communicate a programme of reformation to his father in America. It is an idle conceit, unworthy of a Professor in a Baptist Theological School, and incredible to anybody but mere partisans. But Thomas Campbell, it seems, was following in the track of the Sandemanians, however we may account for it. Prof. Whitsitt is determined to have it so. *But this is not true.* Were the Sandemanians the only people who, about that time, began to speak words of protest against the despotism of creeds? By no means. The Baptists in England, not less than their brethren in Scotland, were no advocates of creeds. To this day, they refuse to be bound by them; in spite, too, of the great influence of their greatest preacher. The roof under which English Baptists assemble for cooperative work must be broad enough to shelter the different schools of doctrine into which the Baptists of the United Kingdom are divided. It has always been so, as we shall see further along. But will our Professor himself contend for "any standards of belief" other than the

Scriptures? Have American Baptists any such "standard"? Standard is our Professor's own word. To have scruples about the use of "human standards" of belief, he regards as proof of Sandemanian heresy! If this is so, let our Baptist brethren cease prating about their fidelity to the Bible as "the only standard."

But Thomas Campbell's position, as against creeds, was no mere vague war-cry, or "glittering generality." He clearly defined what he meant by taking the Bible as the only "standard." Sandemanians and Scotch Baptists inveighed against creeds, but themselves followed the creed-principle. Prof. Whitsitt knows full well that a creed does not need to be written. These parties made their unwritten articles a test of church fellowship, no less exactingly than other sects their written creeds. This cannot be denied. It is this which explains their separatists fecundity. But Thomas Campbell began by guarding against separatism, as far as anything can be guarded against in this imperfect human world. Nothing ought to be made *a test of fellowship*, said he, which is not enjoined by our Lord Jesus Christ; either *in express precept* or by *good and valid precedent.* This is what taking the Bible as the only "standard" meant to him. This is not Sandemanianism, but apostolical Christianity. It came not from Greville Ewing or the Scotch Baptists, but from the New Testament. The first attempt to build on this foundation, thus clearly outlined, since the days of the early church, was made in this new world by Thomas and Alexander Campbell. Let him that denies, show his authority.

The Professor several times intimates that the Sandemanians (including of course the Scotch Baptists) denied any divine influence, outside the gospel testimony, in the production of faith. *This is not true.* It is a stale charge and ought not to be repeated by any writer who desires the respect of truth-loving men. Touching this question, Robert Sandeman himself shall speak first. He is quoted as follows, by A. Campbell, in the *Harbinger* for 1835, p. 356:

> *Two men may be employed with equal diligence in studying the Scriptures, and with equal seriousness in praying for divine assistance; the one may come to know the truth, and the other may grope in the dark all his life-time. Now if we admit this, why is it so? Here is the answer: Faith comes not by any human endeavor, or the use of any means, even under the greatest advantages that men can enjoy:* **but of that same sovereign good pleasure which provided the grand thing to be believed.** (Vol. 2, London, 1768, p. 191.)

This is plain enough. Indeed it could not be otherwise, for Sandeman was a Calvinist, and Calvinism means the production of faith by the divine sovereignty.

Let Archibald McLean speak for the Scotch Baptists:

> *This knowledge and belief of the truth as it is in Jesus, though a duty incumbent on all who hear the gospel, is nevertheless **the special gift of God**, being the effect of divine teaching by means of the word, and peculiar to the elect. (Commission, p. 72.)*
>
> *The power of Jesus in giving sight to the blind man, made him instantly sensible that he saw, and left no room for reasoning on the subject; even so, when the import and evidence of the truth **shines into the heart by the enlightening spirit,** it has at once the double effect of **producing belief**, and the consciousness of it. (Ibid., p. 82.)*
>
> *The testimony of conscience will be more or less explicit, according to the degree of faith which is the subject of it; even as faith itself is weak or strong in proportion to the degree of light and evidence with which the gospel **by the Spirit shines into the mind**, which is the foundation of both. (Ibid. p. 85.)*

Andrew Fuller himself testifies that these men believed in divine influence in order to faith. In his review of McLean, (Appendix to his *Gospel Worthy*, etc. p. 208) he writes as follows:

> *That there is a divine influence on the soul, which is necessary to spiritual perception and belief, as being the cause of them, those with whom I am now reasoning will admit. **The only question is, in what order these things are caused?** Whether the Holy Spirit causes the mind, while carnal, to discern and believe spiritual things, and thereby renders it spiritual [the position of Sandeman and McLean]; or whether he imparts a holy susceptibility, and relish for the truth, in consequence of which we discern its glory, and embrace it... The latter appears to me to be the truth.*

It is hard to have patience with those Baptist scribes, who not only misrepresent Sandeman, McLean, and all the Scotch Baptists, but who are so ignorant of the writings of their own Fuller, as not to know that he concedes the truth which they are making bold to deny. Sandeman, McLean, and Fuller were all Calvinists, and agreed that faith is possible only to the elect. They agreed further, as every man knows who knows anything about it, that saving or justifying faith *is the belief of the gospel;*

or, to put it in Fuller's own words, "the persuasion of the truth of what God hath said." They agreed also that this *belief* or *persuasion* of the truth implies a *spiritual perception* of its relations to the soul's needs, and an acceptance of it, as free and full and adequate for the soul's salvation. They differed, as Fuller expressly says, about the order in which faith and regeneration are caused. Fuller thought faith was the effect of prior regeneration, and Sandeman, McLean, and all that school, held that regeneration is the effect of faith. This was the gist of the whole controversy. To pretend to anything else, is either to confess ignorance of the facts, or to disregard them entirely. When Sandeman spoke of faith in connection with justification as "the bare belief of the bare truth," he only affirmed that justification is grounded, not upon a holiness of heart implied in believing, but upon the believing itself, as separated from that holiness which is the immediate effect of it. The same position has already been noticed in McLean's treatise on the Commission. Neither Sandeman or McLean thought of faith otherwise than as the "special gift of God," and dependent upon an exercise of divine sovereignty.

The general want of fairness which pervades Mr. Whitsitt's book may be indicated by a single quotation:

> *In the year 1816, he was able to excite a small controversy by a discourse on "The Law," before the Redstone Association, where, in keeping with his Sandemanian principles, he thought the preaching of the gospel was sufficient to produce "the bare belief of the bare truth," and therefore maintained that it was unnecessary and reprehensible to persuade men by the terrors of the Lord.*

Now, as a matter of fact, the phrase "bare belief of the bare truth," is not in the Sermon on The Law referred to. Nor is anything said about faith, which implies such a conception of it. Besides, this sermon shows that Mr. Campbell's view of divine influence was then what is generally called the orthodox view. A single quotation will prove this:

> *The Christian dispensation is called "the ministration of the Spirit," and accordingly everything in the salvation of the church is accomplished **by the immediate energy of the Spirit**. ... He was to convince the world of sin, of righteousness, and judgment; **Not by applying the law of Moses, but the facts concerning Christ, to the consciences of the people**. ... The Spirit **accompanying** the words which the apostles preached [most orthodox phrase], would convince the world of sin, etc., ... so that Christ, and not the law, was the Alpha and Omega of their sermons; and this the **Spirit***

made effectual to the salvation of thousands.

The intimation that Mr. C., in this discourse, regarded the preaching of "the terrors of the Lord" as a reprehensible procedure, is also without a particle of foundation. The "terrors of the Lord" are far more clearly exhibited in the gospel than they were under the law of Moses. And it is the preaching of "the law," instead of the gospel, as a means of conversion, that is specially reprobated in this sermon. How a Baptist editor — I do not now remember of what paper — could speak of the Professor's book as without a blunder in historical statement, must seem passing strange to all who have cared to acquaint themselves with the real history.

Mr. W. quotes Dr. Richardson as saying that "before the family departed from Rich Hill, he had been much pleased with the works of Archibald McLean, especially his work on 'the Commission' of which he was wont ever after to speak in the highest terms." "This incident," he says, "is important to the student of his life and changes." But, if "this incident" turns out to be spurious, then a link in the Professor's fantastic chain of historical caricature is lost forever. What Prof. Richardson really says, is this: "He *seems*, in addition, about this time to have read, and to have been much pleased with the works of Archibald McLean, especially his work on the Commission, &c., &c." Dr. R. says he *seems* to have read. This, of course, is an expression of uncertainty; but it suits Mr. W.'s whim to speak of it as *absolute history*. Now, there is the very best authority for saying that Dr. Richardson was, in this instance, mistaken. In a letter to Elder W. Jones, Scotch Baptist, of London, Mr. Campbell himself speaks of his first acquaintance with McLean's writings as follows:

> *I may, therefore, indirectly be indebted to Archibald McLean, for example, much more than I am aware.* ***A few years after my immersion****, I read one volume of his tracts, and I do not know that I have ever read but his Review of Wardlaw's Lectures, his Reply to Fuller, a Defense of Believer's Baptism, The Substance of two Discourses preached on Faith, at Kingston-upon-Hull, and a Treatise on the Commission. Sometime after my separation from the Presbyterian connection and my immersion into the ancient faith, a Mr. John Boyle, of Ireland, with whom I formed a slight acquaintance in Scotland, once an Episcopal parson, but then converted by John Walker, of Dublin, to Separatism, made me a visit, and presented to me a volume of the above tracts, and* ***thus***

introduced me to a knowledge of the name of McLean. (*Millennial Harbinger,* 1835. P. 304).

From this, it is perfectly clear that, at the time of writing this letter to Elder Jones, Mr. Campbell had no recollection of having read anything from McLean at an earlier date than the one here mentioned. Dr. Richardson was therefore mistaken in his hypothetical conclusion referred to by Mr. Whitsitt; and the significant "incident," of which the latter makes so much, vanishes from history.

The following characteristic paragraph may excite a smile, or a frown, according to the momentary mood in which the reader shall chance to find himself:

> *In case the representations made by Prof. Richardson are complete, the revolution which took place in Alexander's mind, by which he became a subject of Sandeman in the matter of faith, began in the month of October, 1811, and was completed in the month of March, 1812. In connection with it, he carried forward a correspondence with his father, perhaps chiefly for the purpose of showing him deference. The harmless old gentleman was incapable of rendering him any assistance in his enterprises, but it was in his power to offer a deal of resistance in case he was not duly coddled and conciliated; As on every other occasion, Thomas Campbell played the role of a convenient echo. It is surprising to witness the readiness with which he could repeat at first blush such Sandemanian watch-words as "the bare belief of the naked truth," and affirm, against the convictions of a life-time, that this involuntary, unavoidable faith was sufficient to procure salvation.*

The estimate here offered of the character and intellectual qualifications of the elder Campbell need cause no surprise to anyone. It is not the judgment of a student of the facts, sincerely expressed, but the careless deliverance of an unfriendly critic, utterly misled by his sectarian prejudices. In the quotations made from Thomas Campbell by Dr. Richardson, to which Prof. W. has here referred us, he expresses very definitely his conception of faith in the following words:

> *The full and firm persuasion, then, or hearty belief of the Divine testimony concerning Jesus, comprehensively considered as above defined, is that faith, in its proper and primary acceptation to which the promises and privileges of salvation are annexed. See Peter's confession and the recognitions of John in his first epistle.*

> *"Thou art the Christ the Son of the Living God." "Whosoever believeth that Jesus is the Christ is born of God;" "Who is he that overcometh the world, but he that believeth that Jesus is the Son of God."*

We are content to stand by this definition of faith today, however men may choose to speak of it as Sandemanianism, or to scoff at it as heresy. It would have been perfectly satisfactory, as a definition, to Andrew Fuller, though it may not satisfy such modern Baptists as are more in sympathy with Methodists and "Salvationists" than with their own greatest denominational leader. The expression, "bare belief of the naked truth," which Prof. W. quotes, is put by Thomas Campbell *into the mouth of an objector, and not given as his own conception of the subject.* His statement of his own position, I have given above, in his own words. As to the question whether faith is voluntary or involuntary, little need be said here. It is manifestly one or the other, according to the point of view from which the question is put; and that without regard to any particular theological system. A man cannot believe at will, as everyone knows. And yet a man's beliefs are not independent of his will. A man, let us say, wants to know truth, wills to know it, and bends all his energies of mind and heart to the task of finding it. This whole process is in the highest degree voluntary; but in the act of believing, in deciding what truth is, the final step is determined by the testimony, and may, therefore, be described as involuntary. To men like our professor, this may seem to make the whole matter of believing an intellectual process. Well, is the primary element of faith an act of the mind? Or is it a mere sentiment? An unexplained impulse of the emotions? Which? The scriptural use of the word *belief* stamps upon faith indelibly the nature of the intellect, rather than that of the sensibilities. Not but that, in the larger meaning of the term, as I have already explained, much more than this is included, but that the primary act of saving faith is the mind's acceptance of the testimony concerning Christ; and, consequently, Christ himself, as Savior and Lord. The New Testament writers do not employ words with the cast-iron fixedness of theologians, but with the flexibility and freedom characteristic of common men, in the full exercise of their common sense. So, while the primary element in faith is intellectual, in its larger meaning, and wider scope, it includes also the heart and the life. I may quote a few words here from a sermon preached in the Fourth Baptist Church, St. Louis, Mo., by Rev. L.S. Piker. The text was Hebrews 11:6. I quote from the *Globe-Democrat* of Sept. 10th, 1888.

Faith is founded upon evidence. The intelligent, thinking Christian has, for his faith in God, abiding internal and abounding external evidence. Faith has never been unobjectionably defined. Definition, according to the scholarly Broadus, teaches of what elements an idea, as a whole, is composed... To define faith is no easy matter, as it is too simple to admit of simplifying.

*The **primary part** of faith, according to the text, is to believe that God is... Thus far, a person might believe and still not exercise saving faith. To believe that God **is**, meets a scriptural demand, but not the entire demand for salvation.*

I have quoted these words simply to show that when a Baptist preacher undertakes to expound faith, he is compelled to admit the intellectual ground of it, and to bear witness to the fact that it "is founded upon evidence." It is only when they want to inveigh against Sandemanianism that Baptist preachers and Professors transfer faith quite away from the realm of the intellect to that of the emotions. The simple fact is that, at the *ground* of all emotional experiences and moral determinations embraced in faith, is the decision of the intellect. In its narrower and more elementary sense, it is the mind's "persuasion of the truth of what God hath said," while in the more comprehensive sense, it embraces trust in Christ, and that solemn commitment of the soul to him, which can only be superinduced by means of it.

The entire representation contained in the seventh and eighth chapters of Prof. Whitsitt's book invites sharp criticism. Even Baptist reviewers have not hesitated to express the opinion that there are insinuations here which are not warranted by a candid survey of the facts. The eighth chapter bears the subtitle, "Mr. Campbell's Perversion to Sandemanianism," but it would have more exactly expressed its real character to have named it "Prof. Whitsitt's perversion of History to partisan purposes." He tells us truly that Thomas Campbell proposed to his followers (?), as a basis for action the following motto: "Where the Scriptures speak, we speak; where they are silent, we are silent." He is kind enough to admit that this was an excellent ideal. Indeed he says it was "a neat and popular expression of the fundamental principle of Mr. Greville Ewing." But strangely enough, he immediately adds that "it is nothing more than what is professed in fact, if not in form, by every sect of religious worshipers in Christendom." However, he is careful to say that, "in the mouth of Thomas Campbell, it probably signified nothing more important than 'When Mr. Ewing speaks, we speak; and when he is silent, we are silent.' ... But whether the father or the son should be awarded the credit of this taking of the expression of *the leading principle of Ewing*" — yet only what is professed by *every sect of worshipers in Christendom* — he thinks, may not be easily determined. True, the son was in Scotland, when the father first employed it, but, then, it is naively suggested that he may have had knowledge of the whole business,[284] and may have mapped out, under Ewing's direction, perhaps — who knows? — the order in which each successive step should be taken in the far away regions of the New World! Of course, the object of this is to minimize the work of the elder Campbell, but more especially to suggest a possible connection of his movements here with the Sandemanian tenets of Greville Ewing on the other side of the sea. But even Alexander Campbell, it seems, was not destined to lead, uninterruptedly, the movement which he is supposed to have, in a sense, originated. Both the Campbells, Prof. Whitsitt is anxious to have us believe, were perfectly content with the "aspersion" they had received in infancy. The drift towards immersion in the little church at Brush Run was due to others; the Campbells were carried forward by a current which they were powerless to control. Let us see how it was done.

Mr. Campbell, in his reminiscences, which I have freely quoted, speaks of his investigation of the baptismal question in such a way as to make the impression that it followed immediately his talk with Dr. Riddle concerning certain words in his father's Declaration and Address, and that he continued it without intermission, until he reached the conviction, not only that infant baptism was unauthorized, but that the only admissible form of the ordinance was immersion. This, however, does not appear to have been quite the case. He seems indeed to have thrown aside, after having read them, the works in favor of infant baptism, which had been sent him, disgusted with their fallacious reasonings, and utterly dissatisfied with the Pedo-baptist position. But the final investigation, in which he decided the whole question in the light of the Greek Testament, took place at a somewhat later date. During this interval, his mind seems to have remained in a state of relative indecision. Nothing was more natural. The things pressing upon him chiefly were the emancipation of men's minds from the bondage of creeds, and the tyranny of church establishments not authorized in the word of God, and also the development of a true and trustworthy basis for Christian fellowship and cooperation in the Lord's work. Baptism was a mooted question, and the agitation of it seemed to promise strife rather than the

---

[284] See Appendix.

unity which he had at heart. Naturally, he moved slowly in a matter so fraught with danger. Meantime, there was constant study of the Scriptures, and inevitably more or less discussion in the little community now embarked in a career of reformation. At the first communion service after the organization of the church, it was noticed that three members — Joseph Bryant, Margaret Fullerton, and Abraham Altars — did not partake of the emblems. On inquiry, it appeared that they had none of them been baptized; as Dr. Richardson expresses it, "none of them had received baptism at all in any of its so-called forms." (Memoirs, page 372). After interviews, resulting in a common understanding, Thomas Campbell immersed them. But, of course, the question once fairly before the little church, discussion was not to be avoided. Nor was it desirable that it should be. Dr. Richardson casually mentions that these discussions continued to be kept up during the absence of Alexander Campbell on a preaching tour of some weeks. Prof. Whitsitt lays hold of these circumstances to concoct a tale which no one is likely to believe, and of which he himself should be thoroughly ashamed. He represents Joseph Bryant and James Foster as having been very active in urging the immersionist view. Joseph Bryant especially, needed to be conciliated. He was a very important personage. Indeed, Prof. Whitsitt conjectures that he "was already recognized as an eligible match for Miss Dorothea Campbell, to whom he was united in marriage about twenty months later." Under such circumstances it was not easy to resist him. It began to look as if the church at Brush Run was "going to pieces." "Alexander now perceived that speedy action must be had, else their cause was lost."

"If Bryant and the majority of the little community at Brush Run" — so Prof. Whitsitt gravely writes — "could have been induced to tolerate aspersion, it is probable that the Campbells would never have found it convenient to leave the side of the sprinkling Sandemanians."

And this — shall we believe it? — is what passes with some Baptists for history! A more unwarranted imputation of unworthy motives, it is safe to say, has never been uttered. Suppose that the discussion which occurred under the circumstances here mentioned did have something to do with the thorough investigation of the subject by Alexander Campbell which unmistakably followed, what of that? As to the agitation in the church, and the signs of a general disintegration here intimated, nothing apparently could be farther from the fact. Concerning the state of the church at this very time, Dr. Richardson writes as follows:

> *These religious meetings were sources of great enjoyment. Warmly attached to one another for the truth's sake, and sympa-*

thizing with each other in their trials and religious experiences, they sermed to be of one heart and of one soul. The Bible was their daily study, and they came to the assembly, like bees to a hive, laden with the sweet lessons of instruction it afforded, and ready to say in the language of the Psalm they had sung at their organization:

    "God is the Lord, who, unto us
    Hath made light to arise."

But Prof. Whitsitt, full of his own absurd fantasies, passes all this unnoticed. His role is that of the small pettifogger, and, it must be confessed, he has played it not unskillfully. A man may be forgiven much, who writes or speaks in the heat of theological debate, but Prof. Whitsitt has no such excuse. He has written deliberately, "with malice," it may be said, "and aforethought." To seriously ask us to receive, as history, the things which he has here written, must be regarded as the climax of effrontery. Mr. Campbell's long and faithful Christian life places his memory beyond the reach of such petty, partisan attempts to darken it with dishonor. And yet, it is to be regretted that the rancor and bigotry, which assailed him with all sorts of detraction during his life, could not, now that he has gone, reverently leave his character to the final decision of Him who is the Judge both of the living and the dead. In this work of detraction, Prof. Whitsitt is ingenious, after a sort, but he is far from ingenuous. The facts given by Dr. Richardson are explained out of his own perverse fancy in such way as to give plausible coloring to a picture which is too unlike the reality to be even a good caricature. It is needless to follow him, item by item, in this part of his work. It would be ungrateful toil, and, happily, there is not the least reason for its performance. As a single example, however, of this character of work, the following is offered.

It is said: "Alexander rejected for a while the conceit of Ewing and the Sandemanians, that faith is nothing other than mere belief, *which is produced by testimony alone, without reference to the regenerating grace of God."* And farther down on the same page, we find this: "The 7th of April 1811, is the latest date on which, according to his biographer, he was willing to affirm that faith is of the operation of God, and an effect of almighty power and *regenerating grace."*

Now the untheological reader will utterly fail to appreciate, or even to perceive, the exquisite touch of our historian's art, as here exhibited. His conclusion will be prompt, and free from any misgiving, that, according to Dr. Richardson, Mr. Campbell's chosen biographer, the latter denied, from the date here mentioned, all divine agency in the production of faith, and rejected outright the grace of God in regeneration. But such a conclusion is far from the truth. Mr. Campbell always believed that regeneration, or change of heart, is of the grace of God, *through faith.* But the thing which Mr. C. never believed after the aforementioned date, is the unscriptural and irrational assumption that *"faith is the effect of almighty power and regenerating grace:"* Notice the two predicates: (1) faith is the effect of omnipotent power, (2) it is the effect of regeneration, or follows regeneration. Of course, Alexander Campbell, through his long life, rejected both these unreasonable and unbiblical assumptions. But Dr. Richardson, in the very connection referred to by Mr. W., is careful to say that he always *"retained the idea of a divine interposition, but came to regard it as a providential agency, rather than as a direct operation of the Spirit, as held by popular parties.* Thus the velvet touch of the accomplished caricaturist is exposed to vulgar eyes! Pity that manly and candid Baptists, who love truth and adore the Savior, should be in danger of "perversion" from one who seems to imagine he is doing God service by offering insult to the living, and defaming the memory of the dead.

But, touching the relation of testimony to faith as here referred to, and as held by Mr. Campbell, a few words may not be out of place. It is true that Mr. Campbell always maintained the necessity of testimony in order to faith. He saw clearly, or at least thought he saw clearly, that, between the divine testimony concerning Jesus, and the faith in him, which saves the soul, there is a certain fixed and definite connection, grounded evermore in the very nature of the soul itself. To give the passages in the New Testament in which this connection is positively taught, or fairly indicated, would be to transcribe no small portion of the book. This conception, which is biblically true, by a hundred unmistakable passages, is beyond all doubt a demand of reason as well. The faith which saves, if Paul may be believed, "Comes by hearing the word of God." If John understood himself at all, it is the product of the divine testimony. Listen to his words: "It is the Spirit that bears witness, because the Spirit is the truth. For there are three who bear witness, the Spirit, and the water, and the blood; and the three agree in one. If we receive the witness of men, the witness of God is greater; for the witness of God is this, that he hath borne witness concerning his Son. He that believeth on the Son of God hath the witness in him; he that believeth not God hath made him a liar; because he hath not believed in the witness God hath borne concerning his Son." (1 John 5:7-11, R. V.)

Does Prof. Whitsitt imagine that the recognition of the necessary relation between testimony and faith is a denial of God's providence, or the Spirit's agency? He writes, indeed, as if he were disturbed by some such fantasy. But it is not to be thought this disturbance is real. He knows better. He only seeks to mislead, concerning Mr. Campbell and the Disciples, those who do not know better; namely, a great many Baptists, and, perhaps, some who are not Baptists, but who are only too willing to believe an evil report against those who are not in ecclesiastical affiliation with themselves. Will Prof. Whitsitt undertake to say that anyone has ever believed in Christ without having heard the gospel? Will he assert that, where the gospel is preached, faith is "of the almighty power, and regenerating grace of God," independent of divine testimony, through the word? He will assert no such thing. It is too late in the day for college professors to stultify themselves by affirming such an absurdity. If there is one thing more than another which this age demands of its religious teachers, it is that no insult shall be offered to the most certain judgments of a trained and reverent intellect. It was otherwise when Alexander Campbell began his great work, but it shall not be otherwise anymore until the Lord comes to judge the world. The spirit of mysticism and fetishism is well-nigh exorcised now, in Christian lands, from all human souls. And it is well that such is the case. It has had sway quite long enough. Intelligent Christians will maintain the fact of divine agency, and the necessity of divine truth and testimony, in order to faith and regeneration, henceforth to the end of the world.

Prof. Whitsitt is unwilling to give the least credit of originality to the Campbells. They always copied from someone else. They were only slavish followers of Greville Ewing, at one time, and of Archibald McLean at another. In the matter of "baptism for remission of sins" the impression is at first sought to be made that it was derived from McLean. But nothing can be more absurd. McLean positively taught, as was heretofore stated, that justification follows immediately the act of believing so as to antedate not only all obedience to ordinances, but even the holy disposition of the soul itself, which he regarded as the first effect of faith. Otherwise, says McLean, it could not be said: "He justifieth the ungodly." But McLean has "so guarded his utterances," says Prof. Whitsitt, "that it might be in the power of an opponent to affirm that he was not a thorough-paced advocate of the theory of baptismal remission." No doubt, McLean guarded very carefully his utterances, to the end that no one should have grounds to misrepresent him. But, alas! What watchfulness can thoroughly anticipate and shut off the malign distortions of theological partisans! Men like our Professor defy the most conscientious attempts to guard against the perversion of their utterances. But while McLean guarded his utterances carefully, if we may credit Prof. Whitsitt, it was not so with a certain "Scotch Baptist Church" in the city of New York. This church sent out, it seems, a sort of circular letter, which is supposed to have been "forwarded to all the Sandemanian churches of the immersion observance in America." This letter, it is contended, boldly avowed "the same view regarding the design of baptism to which the Campbells later gave their adhesion… The same texts, which the sect of Disciples (or Campbellites) are in the habit of setting forward, are produced in this pamphlet, and handled in much the same way, in order to support the conclusion that baptism was designed for the remission of sins."

This is only a half-truth; indeed, it is scarcely that. The texts of Scripture, which speak of "the uses and purposes for which baptism was appointed," are indeed carefully given, and their importance is duly insisted upon; but the conclusion that "baptism is for remission of sins" is conspicuous only by its entire absence. If Bro. Baxter, in his life of Scott, has intimated the contrary, then he was mistaken. *There is no baptism for remission of sins in this New York letter.* What was Professor Whitsitt thinking about, when he read — or did he read? — the following paragraph in said letter?

> *No one who has been in the habit of considering it [baptism] merely as an ordinance [or rite] can read these passages with attention without being surprised at the wonderful powers, and qualities, and effects, and uses, which are there apparently [please notice this word] ascribed to it… If the language employed respecting it, in many of the passages were to be taken literally [please note this] it would import that remission of sins is to be obtained by baptism, that escape from the wrath to come is effected in baptism, that men are born children of God by baptism, etc., etc… All these things, **if all the passages before us were construed literally** would be ascribed to baptism. And it was a literal construction of these passages which led professed Christians in the early ages to believe that baptism was necessary to salvation. Hence arose infant baptism, and other customs equally unauthorized. And, from a like literal construction of the words of the Lord Jesus, at the last supper, arose the awful notion of transubstanti-*

ation.[285]

Now the careful reader has not failed to see (1), that certain things are here said to be taught concerning baptism, *provided*, that the words of the texts referred to are to be construed literally: but, (2), that the literal construction is clearly repudiated as untenable. How the authors *did* construe these passages, will appear from their own words, as follows:

> *It is for the churches of God, therefore, to consider well, whether it does not clearly and forcibly appear from what is said of baptism in the passages before us, taken each in its proper connection, that baptism was appointed as an institution **strikingly significant** of several of the most important things relating to the kingdom of God; whether it was not in baptism that men professed by deed, as they had already done by word, to have the remission of sins through the death of Jesus Christ, and to have a firm persuasion of being raised from the dead through him and after his example; whether it was not in baptism that they **put off** the ungodly character and its lusts, and put on the new life of righteousness; whether it was not in baptism that they **professed to have their sins washed away, through the blood** of the Lord and Savior, etc.*

I need not quote more fully. It is absolutely clear that the church which sent forth this letter entertained precisely the same view of the design of baptism which is held by the Associated Baptists throughout this country, at the present time. Baptism, on the part of the recipient, was a profession in act, of having received *already* the remission of sins; as respects the divine purpose in requiring it; it was intended to set forth symbolically the cleansing of the soul from sin through the blood of Christ. This, and only this, was in it. If they dwelt with more emphasis upon its importance than Baptists are now expected to do, the fact may be explained by considering that they were not under the same necessity of guarding their words to keep off suspicion of sympathy with the heresies of the Disciples and New Testament Christians. This whole matter is conspicuously plain and simple.

Concerning Prof. Whitsitt's insistent efforts to depreciate and belittle the Campbells as men of intellectual power, nothing more than a word of reference is here necessary. Thomas Campbell, he tell us, was only a "convenient echo;" and if ever Alexander had an original idea, he "took

---

[285] [Items in brackets in this quotation were inserted by Mr. Longan]

pains to avoid giving expression to it in such of his writings as have been submitted to the inspection of the public."

No doubt our Professor needed to let off the gall which was in him, and if such words as these answered that purpose, we need make no complaint. If, in face of the intelligence of the age, he can choose to express himself in this fashion, it is his affair, not ours. No friend of the Campbells need care to say one word in reply.

It might be well to have a thoughtful comparison of the views of the Disciples and Baptists. Perhaps, someday, we shall have it. But Prof. Whitsitt's book adds nothing valuable to the literature of this long, and too often bitter, controversy.

Against the Baptist people, as such, I have no hard words to utter; I recall no personal grievances, leaving bitter memories, which might justify, even on the world's principle of retaliation, any harsh or unkind criticism. I owe them nothing but love. There is not a man of them all, who follows sincerely and reverently the Lord Jesus, albeit, like the rest of us, oftentimes, at a distance, and with unsteady step, that I do not unfeigned love for Jesus' sake.

There is not a single such follower of Christ among them that I do not habitually recognize and treat as a brother in the common faith. He may cling to much "foolishness" in theology, or dwell with fond delight on certain pietistic superstitions connected with his "experience "of God's grace in his soul — a thing he is quite sure to do — and it makes no difference at all. If he bear the "image and superscription" of the Lord Jesus, God has received him, with all his imperfections of knowledge and life, and who am I, that I should reject one of these "little ones" for whom Christ died? Upon this principle the Disciples have always acted. A letter from a Baptist church has always been a sufficient passport to our fellowship. It has mattered nothing at all that there has been no reciprocity in our relations with them. We have remained true to our divine law of affiliation throughout all the keen controversies and un-fraternal imputations of evil heresies, in the seventy-five years (speaking in round numbers) which have passed away since our movement first began to assume definite shape. To this principle we shall be true here-after, as we have been heretofore, whatever the coming years may have in store for us.

But why should our Baptist brethren — any of them — put on airs in talking about us? Why write articles in their papers, or books even, whose chief characteristic is the partisan's bitter sneer? Are we not every whit their equals in whatever gives prestige and power to a body of

Christian believers? Nay, taking into account our briefer history as a distinct people, are we not rapidly gaining upon them in all the elements of denominational greatness? If I may speak foolishly, "in this confidence of boasting," as it were, I would say that it concerns us not at all — save for the honor of our common Christianity — what the narrow-minded zealots of any sect in Christendom may choose to say about us. The time has gone by when the *odium theologicum* could be used successfully as a weapon against us. Save for the honor of the Lord's cause, so often put to shame by his professed friends, there is no reason why we should give ourselves a moment's anxiety over any of these things. But for this, we could listen patiently to Prof. Whitsitt, and all the rest, as long as they find comfort in pouring out the bitterness that is in them. For the harm it does us we are not greatly concerned.

But who are these Baptist people, from whose ranks someone arises ever and anon, "speaking great swelling words of vanity?" What is *their* "origin?" What *their* history? Was John the Baptizer their founder? Have they had a continuous existence through all the centuries since? There are indeed some partisans among them who would fain have men think so. Their real scholars do not pretend any such thing. They know better, and are candid enough to tell what they know.

But really, now, how shall we define a Baptist? How shall we differentiate him? In point of fact he is a vague specimen. There are General Baptists, Particular Baptists, and "Scottish Baptists," in the mother country; there are Missionary Baptists and Anti-missionary Baptists; Baptists that are Calvinists, and Baptists that believe in the freedom of the human will; to say nothing of Seventh Day Baptists, of Six Principle Baptists, and of German Baptists, or Tunkers, all here in our own America. The reader sees the difficulty. To which of these half dozen sects, all claiming to be "Baptists" par excellence, shall we accord the honor of calling it the Baptist Church? And what are the relations of these Baptist sects to each other? Do they mutually give and receive letters of commendation? Do they break bread with each other in the Lord's Supper? Not to any great extent, certainly. But our special anxiety is to find the Baptist Church. Can Prof. Whitsitt locate it? Will he give us its metes and bounds, so that we can speak advisedly in regard to it? He will scarcely undertake so hopeless a task. Or, if he should see that no aggregation of Baptist local communities can be called a *church,* in the New Testament sense of the term, and so prefer to speak of *Baptist churches,* and of the "Baptist denomination," would he be so kind as to indicate clearly the latter's exact comprehension? How many of these sects, popularly called *Baptists*, are outside of the Baptist denomination, as Prof. Whitsitt would employ that expression? If a member of Spurgeon's Baptist church of the free communion "observance," for instance, should offer a letter to a Baptist church of the close communion "observance," here in America, would it be received at par value in such church? Or, if a Free Will Baptist should bring a letter from his church in New England to the Baptist church in Louisville, in which Prof. Whitsitt has his membership, how would he be received? Would his letter be received as coming from "a sister church of the same faith and order?" Do Primitive Baptists and Missionary Baptists mutually recognize each other's baptism and sound Baptistic order and orthodoxy? Do they give letters to, and receive letters from, each other, as of the same faith and order?

Of course, an outsider cannot know all about the "usage" in such cases, but he need not wholly repress his curiosity. It is laudable to desire information upon doubtful points, when circumstances give importance to them. Now of course the "Scottish Baptists" are not Baptists at all, but only "Sandemanians of the immersion observance." And of course we are to suppose that Prof Whitsitt would not think of receiving into fellowship a Scotch Baptist without a formal renunciation of his Sandemanianism. He might, perhaps, go behind his letter, and examine him on his "experience." But that would amount to nothing. A genuine Scotch Baptist can tell quite as good a Baptistic experience as Prof. Whitsitt himself; and this our learned professor very well knows. He is as sound on depravity, on divine sovereignty, on the influence of the Spirit, on personal election, as the soundest professor in any Baptist Seminary in America. He cannot be shut out by any of these tests. Call him "a Sandemanian of the immersion observance," and refuse him fellowship on that ground. You must do that, or receive him.

But what then? If you receive him you recognize his Sandemanian heresy, or at least account it no bar to fellowship (which is indeed the only sensible thing to be done in such a case), and if you do not receive him, you violate what is said to be a fundamental usage of the Baptist people, which has obtained among them, with more or less uniformity, from time immemorial, namely, not to make speculative differences — such differences as affect not "a true experience of God's grace in the soul" — a bar to fellowship. Is a man less a Baptist because he is a Calvinist or an anti-Calvinist? Is he less or more a Baptist because he doubts the divine origin, or sound expediency of Missionary Societies? Baptists were not wont in the old days to regard these questions as presenting an insurmountable bar to fellowship. At the time of the division between missionary and anti-missionary Baptists here in the great West, the position of the missionary party gave them an advantage which served them a most excellent purpose while the work of separation was going on. They said, "Let us have no quarrel over this matter. Let our churches be free to follow their convictions. Let the individual members in every church have the same freedom." This was sound and scriptural. It was common prudence as well. Nay, it was more; it was the shrewdest sort of strategy. That the missionary leaven would finally leaven pretty much the whole Baptist lump, was clear to the far-seeing leaders, provided it could only have time to diffuse itself. If the churches could be held together, while the leavening process was going on, the end was sure. But clearly, in the event of separation, the burden of responsibility would rest with the separatists. The wisdom of these missionary leaders is apparent to everyone now. Call it conscience or strategy, the effect was the same. Multitudes remained in the churches, and finally became good missionary Baptists, who would have gone out so fast that you could not have counted them, if the issue had been too hotly pressed. Indeed, in not a few cases, the majority would have been on the anti-missionary side.

But the point in all this, which concerns the present argument, is the manifest difficulty of ascertaining the conditions which determine a true Baptistic status, in relation both to individuals and churches. Perhaps Professor Whitsitt was not thinking about this difficulty, when he so unceremoniously thrust the whole Scottish Baptist fraternity outside the pale of genuine Baptistism. They do not even belong, in his classification, to what some Baptists are wont, on occasion, to call "the Baptist family." They are only "Sandemanians of the immersion observance." For shame, Prof. Whitsitt! Are not Scotch Baptists as good Christians as Prof. Whitsitt himself? And have they not as much right, if they choose to do so, to call themselves Baptists? There can be no doubt of it, at all. Now the truth we are seeking seems to be this: While Baptists have not been outspoken in denying to speculative differences of the sort we have here referred to the importance which belongs only to questions of fellowship, there has been, nevertheless, to a certain extent, a sort of tacit recognition among them of that great principle. They might, indeed, separate into sects over such differences, but they still remained ***Baptistic sects.*** They belonged in common to the great "Baptist family," and when the Baptist Israel was to be numbered, they were entitled to be counted. So, likewise, when Baptist histories were to be written, their claim to a true Baptistic character was duly recognized. Thus, there are different "orders" of Baptists, but — shall we put it in that way? — only one true Baptistic test; namely, the faith in Christ, and that one faith expressed in immersion, as the one divine form of baptism. Is it this faith, expressed in the one baptism, which is to be regarded as the true and only test of Baptistic status? If so, the "Baptist family" is indeed a large family, or rather a tribe, including several families, as the one Israel of old included the twelve tribes. But is it indeed true that faith in Christ expressed in Christian baptism (immersion) constitutes the one condition of church and Christian fellowship among Baptists? We should hesitate to accept this statement, and yet it is supported by very high Baptist authority. I give for the reader's consideration the following paragraph from the introduction to Orchard's History of the Baptists (Tenth Edition, Nashville, Tenn., 1855).

> *The ground of unity and denominational claim to the people whose Christian characters are detailed, is not the harmony of their creeds or views; this was not **visible or essential in the first age**; but **the bond of union**, among our denomination **in all ages**, has been **faith in Christ**; and that faith **publicly expressed by a voluntary submission to his authority and doctrine in baptism**.* (Introduction, p. 14.)

I give this extract with boldface and italics, just as I find it in the book. The words are those of Mr. Orchard, quoted in an introductory essay, signed with the initials J.H.G., *i.e.*, J.H. Graves, then of Nashville, Tenn. Of course Mr. Graves is presumed to have given his endorsement to the extract by quoting it without objection. But surely he must have hesitated to do this. The canon here laid down is one that reaches very far indeed, and a Baptist of Mr. Graves' school could hardly accept it as a statement of fact, if he had, at the time, a clear understanding of the question. But Mr. Orchard doubtless meant what he said. He saw clearly that any plausible attempt to make out a Baptistic succession would depend upon the adoption of a very liberal test of Baptist character; and in the freer and larger spirit of the English Baptists, was satisfied with the rule, as he here gives it. Can we hope to get our American Baptists to see and acknowledge what Mr. Orchard's rule really means, and then to cordially accept it as a sound test of Baptist orthodoxy? If so, it is certain that a great point will have been gained.

But, in point of fact, we should say it is *not* true that the bond of union among Baptists has always, or ever, been what Mr. Orchard represents it to have been. In his desire to make out some sort of Baptistic succession from the days of the apostles, he gives up the Baptist bond of union, as utterly untenable for his purpose, and adopts, outright, that of the Disciples of Christ. "The bond of union among our denomination," he says, "has always been *faith in Christ, and that faith **publicly expressed** by a voluntary submission to has authority and doctrine in baptism*." It is simply impossible to express in words more definitely the view of this subject maintained by the Disciples from the very beginning, only, with us, this bond of union is held to be the test of fellowship for all Christian churches, instead of a denominational, or party test. Mr. Orchard's canon of ecclesiastical fellowship is catholic or Christian, and in no true sense Baptistic. But, as was said a moment since, there seems to have been a sort of undercurrent of conviction that some such rule was demanded by the claim Baptists were constantly setting up to some sort of denominational continuity in history. On any other principle than the broad one here laid down, it was clear that no shadow even of plausibility could be imparted to such a claim. Hence, for the purpose of tracing Baptistic succession, a law of affiliation is laid down as denominational, while, as a matter of fact, the practice among Baptists has always been very different. Are all the sects of Baptists which do positively maintain a separate existence to be counted together as *the Baptist denomination*, as Orchard's rule implies? If so, why not go a step further, and abolish altogether the principle of sect-fellowship on agreement in doctrinal beliefs, and merge all these distinct factions into one single Baptist fraternity, upon the larger and more catholic basis here laid down? It is certain that these Baptist sects are kept apart by their "doctrinal differences," which constitute, therefore, the real bonds of union in Baptist practice, while Mr. Orchard's bond of union is a purely theoretical one, devised for the purpose of giving a sort of logical basis to the plea of Baptistic succession.

So the question returns, Who are the Baptists? By what rule shall we know them? Is the larger faction to be taken as the denomination, and the rest to be regarded as heretical, or, at least, disorderly "offshoots" from the true stock? How is this? And upon the offshoot theory, may it not appear that the "Regulars," who are anti-missionary, are the true Baptists, and that our missionary brethren are only offshoots? I care not to press these questions further. I am sure we shall not be able to decide them. And I am equally sure that Orchard's bond of union, which is that of the Disciples, and not Baptistic at all, will continue to be repudiated in practice by all these Baptist sects for many years to come. But, in any event, it behooves such Baptists as Prof. Whitsitt to say whom he acknowledges as Baptists, and whom he repudiates as heretics, or disorderly offshoots. And, especially, it behooves him to show why the regular, or Primitive Baptists, should not be regarded as in the true line of succession from the Baptist fathers, and himself and brethren as offshoots from the one original Baptistic stem. There was a time, it is safe to say, when three-fourths of the Baptists in America were decidedly opposed to missionary societies, and possibly, to all that is now regarded as distinctively missionary work. This must not be forgotten.

But, if the question of origin and history is to be brought to the front, then the Baptist scribes will have their hands full without stopping to utter naughty gibes at any of their neighbors. Prof. Whitsitt expresses the opinion that the Disciples have never succeeded as Biblical exegetes. What truth there is in this opinion we need not stop here to determine. But how many Baptists are known as exegetes of distinction in the great world of Christian scholarship today? It will be time enough to taunt us with deficiency in this respect, when we shall have had the length of time they have had, and shall show no better results. Old-fashioned Baptist text-preaching is hardly to be taken as a phase of exegetics, but certainly it furnishes a sort of test of Baptist aptitude for exegetical work, in days long past. The writer of this review has heard some strange sermons from Baptist pulpits in his time. One preacher took as a text this verse of Solomon's Song: "*My beloved is gone down in his garden, to the beds of spices to feed in the gardens, and to gather lilies*" (6:2). There was little of exegesis in this case, but the preacher found a stirring, and, for those days, a thoroughly characteristic Baptist sermon in his text. There are Baptist communities today, which would be transported into ecstasies by such a sermon. Another took this text: "*And they called Rebecca, and said unto her, Wilt thou go with this man? And she answered and said, I will go*" (Gen. 24:58). Into this simple text — which was a favorite one with Baptists in those days — the preacher read his whole theory of redemption. Abraham's servant was the preacher of the gospel; Rebecca was the sinner; the camel on which Rebecca rode was the law; when Rebecca veiled herself, and dismounted, at the end of the journey, the preacher saw a most impressive type of a sinner's surrender to Christ, after the law has done its work in his heart! Oh, no! It was not exegesis, certainly; but it was genuine Baptist preaching, of the most popular type, at the time when Alexander Campbell preached his sermon on the law before the Redstone Association. And the fact that the sermon dealt a deathblow to such preaching was doubtless the reason why the Redstone leaders saw heresy in it! The Baptist scribe who knows Baptist history, will be a little chary of reproaches which may provoke even the most good-natured retort along these lines. There never has been a time in the history of the Disciples when their ministry would not compare favorably, in every respect, with that of any Baptist party. This is not boasting, but a simple fact of history; which, however, would not have been mentioned, if the case had not seemed to require it.

But the "origin" of the Baptists! What special cause of gratulation can Baptists find in it? Of course our American Baptists are sprung, for the most part, from English sources. What, then, was the origin of the English Baptists? In a brilliant article on Baptist Theology, printed first in the *Contemporary Review*, and afterwards copied into the *Library Magazine* for June, 1888. Dr. Clifford of England informs us that the first church of General Baptists in England was founded in, or about, 1611, by John Smyth and Thomas Helwyss. "Besides the idea of the spiritual life, they also preached the doctrine of general redemption." "Twenty years afterward," continues Dr. Clifford, "and on the 12th of September, 1633, another Baptist Church of a different type was created at Wopping by secession from the Independent Church, dating back to 1616. Its pastor was John Spillsbury, and its theology was fashioned on the model of that marvelous piece of doctrinal literature, the *Institutes* of John Calvin." From these beginnings have sprung, directly, or indirectly, all the Baptists of Great Britain and the United States. But did John Smyth baptize himself? I cannot tell. His Pedobaptist opponents said that he did, but that may have been prejudice and persecution. The Lord knows what the truth is. Perhaps the world will never know. And the Particular Baptist church of which Spillsbury was pastor — whence did that derive the scriptural baptism? The question cannot be certainly answered. Benedict (*History of the Baptists*, p. 337) admits that much obscurity hangs over the whole matter. He says: "It must be admitted that there is some obscurity respecting the manner in which the ancient immersion of adults, which appears to have been discontinued, was restored, when, after the long night of anti-Christian apostasy, persons were at first baptized on a profession of faith." This remark is made in connection with the Particular Baptists. But concerning the Smyth-Helwyss foundation of General Baptists, he confesses the same uncertainty. Smyth, after embracing Baptist sentiments, had fled to Holland to escape persecution. Now, there were Baptist churches in Holland, but they were as "fantastic" a set of people as any seeker after queer social and religious phenomena could wish to see. "The foreign anabaptists," says Crosby, "were such as denied Christ's having taken the flesh of the Virgin Mary, the lawfulness of magistracy, and such like, which Mr. Smyth and his followers looked on as great errors; so that they could not be thought by him proper administrators of baptism."

Upon the whole, Benedict thinks that Smyth and his followers "first formed themselves into a church, and then appointed two of their number (perhaps Mr. Smyth and Mr. Helwyss) to baptize the rest." He adds, with evident feeling, that "this subject caused considerable uneasiness and reproach to the first Baptists after the Reformation, both general and particular." The rise of the whole Baptist denomination in England and America, in this irregular way, seems to be pretty well assured, and if "origin" is the question, then they are the last people in this country who ought to begin throwing stones at others. Of course, the case of Roger Williams and his Rhode Island Baptist church is well known. The Baptists ought not to press questions of "origin" too zealously, if they do not wish to hear these things referred to as a part of their ecclesiastical inheritance.

But the Scottish Baptists, so zealously traduced by Mr. Whitsitt, were a theologically respectable people, on any showing, compared with the English Baptists before Fuller's day. Listen to this Baptist witness: "The prevailing system of doctrine among the Baptist churches at this period was ultra-Calvinism — a system which denies true faith to be the duty of every one to whom the gospel comes; which consequently must paralyze the efforts of ministers 'to go into all the world, and preach the gospel to every creature'; commanding all men everywhere to repent, at the peril of their souls." Fuller's first, if not his greatest work, was to demolish this prevalent and mischievous antinomianism, as Dr. Clifford styles it. Here Fuller and the Scotch Baptists were one, though they reached the same goal by different routes. If one takes the history of the numerous Baptist sects, and traces them carefully through all changes and metamorphoses, he will find no great reason for the indulgence of that spirit of self-sufficiency and exclusivism, which so markedly characterizes certain Baptist leaders of our time. To barely hint at these things, is all that is possible in this review. One may well hesitate to disagree with Dr. John Duncan, who says, as quoted by Dr. Clifford: "There is only one real heresy. Antinomianism." The reproach of this heresy, both in England and America, the Baptists must be content to bear, beyond any other people. If they are now happily freed from its blighting influence, they are to be sincerely congratulated by all good men. It is only admissible to remind them of these things in order to keep them humble, and prevent them from putting on airs which make them ridiculous. If they will behave themselves hereafter, we do not care to reproach them with the past. May the dear Lord lead them into all truth, in his own time, and in his own way!

CHAPTER VII:
THE RELATION OF THE DISCIPLES OF CHRIST TO ALEXANDER CAMPBELL AND OTHER LEADERS

The Disciples cheerfully acknowledge a debt of gratitude to the Campbells, and other able and excellent men, who led in the work of reformation in the earlier years of this century. Nor do they deny their indebtedness to all the reformers, Baptists and Pedobaptists, of whatever schools of thought. Scarcely a great man has lived and wrought for God, whose labors have not shed light on some of the questions which interest all thoughtful men. The true disciple is thankful for such help, let it come from what source it may. All the men who have sought and found truth we reckon among our spiritual ancestors, although we may reject many of their formulas. The progress from the great apostasy has been slow and toilsome. Those who, from time to time, have attained, under God, to the largest measures of divine reality, have been our greatest bene-factors, and constitute the true succession of reformers, from Wycliffe down to our own day. We agree heartily with Dr. Clifford, when he states the progress of reformation as follows:

> *The all-absorbing question of the 16th century was this — what is the church of the Lord Jesus Christ, and of what persons ought it to consist? Protestantism was the bold rejection of the established and orthodox answer supplied by Romanism to this inquiry; Puritanism qualified and cleansed the answer of Protestantism; Separatism went further, and gave increased sharpness to the answer urged by the Puritans; the Brownists, or Independents, still on the forward march, eliminated the parochial element from church membership, and insisted on the possession of spiritual life. Then came the Baptists and added the obligation of developing the spiritual life into **avowed consciousness** before admission into the church. And inasmuch as the only mode of conscientious speech known in those days was that of separation from those with whom they differed, **away they went, carrying whatever theology they had inherited to their new ecclesiastical home**.*

To complete this statement, and bring down the succession to the present day, it remains to be said, that the Disciples have added to whatever of truth the above named parties had found, the *scriptural basis of fellowship and ecclesiastical unity*, and also given an answer to the question of *personal salvation*, surpassing in clearness and fullness, both of biblical proof and rational exposition, anything known in history since the apostles of our Lord Jesus Christ went home to glory.

And for myself, I may be permitted to say, that of this final advance, I think, there is no reasonable doubt, and that the step thus taken by the Disciples is the longest and best single step since Luther, in the whole series of reformation movements. The true law of ecclesiastic affiliation — namely, the faith in Christ and obedience to his commandments — and the great question of personal salvation — "what shall I do to be saved?" — cleared of all irrelevant and unscriptural issues and alike of all mystic and superstitious fantasies — this is the claim of the Disciples before the world of our day, a claim for which, if just, we can afford to toil, and, if need be, to suffer, till the Lord shall come. We seek not to disparage the work of others, but with our own mission we are quite content. If the Lord shall enable us to be faithful to it, in our day and generation, what more need we desire? Let us be satisfied and thankful.

But what is our true relation to the great and good men to whom we so cheerfully acknowledge our special indebtedness? This is a question of no mean significance in estimating the value of our distinctive plea. It is a question, too, the right answer to which it seems very hard to make clear to our brethren in the various denominational folds. They will pardon us, I trust, for holding very emphatically that the fault is not on our side, or in the cause we plead.

When Luther completed his work, he had not only succeeded in impressing his personal modes of thought and experience upon his contemporaries, who followed immediately in his movement, but he had taken care that these modes of thought, this mould of religious experi-ence, should be perpetuated indefinitely, if possible, to the very end of time. He had bravely rejected the Papal traditions, but he seemed not at all averse to imposing upon his successors, in all the time to come, his own traditions. Grant that he thought his theological ideas identical, for substance, with the original gospel, and that does not at all change the fact. He left an ecclesiastical organism pledged to the maintenance of these theological ideas, and fully equipped for the perpetuation of its own existence without limit as to duration. Nothing short of an ecclesi-astical revolution, similar to that which he had led against Rome, could ever make the church which he may be said to have founded, anything more or better than "The Lutheran Church." Its symbolism was Lutheran throughout, and Luther's articles were bound upon the consciences of his followers, if not *in secula seculorum*, at least to the end of this present world. Luther, it is clear, intended to found a church to perpetuate his own ideas. Doubtless he believed these ideas to be, only in another shape, the gospel of Jesus Christ, but, as was said a moment ago, that does not alter the fact. Luther's church was intended to reflect forever Luther's conception of the Christian religion: the Lutheran articles are bound upon its conscience today.

Now what is here said of Luther is manifestly just as true of Calvin and Wesley. Calvinian articles constitute the doctrinal basis, the ecclesiastical organic law and bond of union, of every Calvinistic church on earth — Presbyterian, Puritan, and Baptist alike. As for Wesley, there is no power in the church he founded to make the slightest change in the "articles of religion" which he fastened irrevocably upon it. Changes of an economical character may be made by a general conference, but it has no right to — it dare not — touch a single article of the Wesleyan faith. These facts speak volumes on the question for the moment before us. Let no reader stop till he sees clearly their whole meaning; otherwise, the differentiation we are seeking to effect will not clearly appear. But concerning Baptists and other congregational communities, it is proper to say that there has ever been a measure of relaxation from the bondage of confessional authority, and yet not that genuine freedom in Christ which suffices to take them out of the general category to which I have here assigned them. In the briefer and less rigid epitomes of doctrine adopted by Baptist churches and associations, the distinctive ideas and traditions of the Baptist fathers of different schools are still more or less faithfully perpetuated.

As respects the Disciples, however, the case is very different. The first thing in our movement was to secure freedom, for all time, from the tyranny of mere confessional authority. The first number of *The Christian Baptist* bore at the front the flag of Christian freedom. At the head of its first page was inscribed this motto:

> *Style no man on earth your Father; for he alone is your Father who is in heaven; and all ye are brethren. Assume not the title of Rabbi; for you have only one Teacher; neither assume the title of Leader; for you have only one Leader, the Messiah.*

This motto sounded the key-note of our reformation. In the mouth of Mr. Campbell these words were not the expression of an aggressive and defiant individualism. Mr. C. was indeed, from the beginning of his public career, an independent thinker and a fearless proclaimer of his assured convictions. But no man felt more profoundly than he the need of mutual toleration and respect, in order to the maintenance of spiritual unity, and a catholic fellowship in the congregations of the living God. What he asserted for himself he accorded freely and unhesitatingly to the humblest disciple in the ranks. The chosen motto was not for himself only, but for all. "Where the Bible speaks he would speak, where the Bible was silent he would be silent," as to authoritative utterance. Nothing should be made a test of fellowship or membership which could not be supported "by express precept or approved precedent," taken from the word of God, and applied in its proper contextual limitations. The follower of the dear Lord was not to be judged on account of his opinions on questions of "doubtful disputation." He recognized the right of untrammeled inquiry, but maintained a broad difference between the gospel of Jesus Christ, having for its content the way of salvation, and the uncertain deductions which constitute the formulas of systematic theology in all the widely conflicting schools. What Christ has bound upon the human soul, in order to its salvation, must be loosed by no human hand. But this binding is either in express precept or good and valid precedent. A condition of salvation is never an inference. The *facts* about Christ, the faith in Christ, the obedience to Christ, the blessings and franchises enjoyed through Christ — these are the topics of the gospel of redemption. He allowed theory its proper place, as the attempt of the human mind to explain rationally the facts and commandments of the gospel, but he sternly denied the right of any disciple to force his personal explanation on the conscience of another. It was a characteristic utterance, when he once affirmed, "God never saved a man for believing a theory, or damned a man for disbelieving one." In the field of religious philosophy the soul is free, but this Christian freedom is not to run into license in speculation, any more than in the corresponding department of conduct or life. It is easy to darken counsel by words without knowledge. Unbridled speculation is, and always has been, an evil of great magnitude in the church of God. We are indeed free to think, but wisdom in the expression of our thought is a true test of usefulness in a disciple of Jesus Christ. So one may theorize — for how can a thinking man keep quite clear of theory? — but his theories are mainly for himself, and must not be bound on other people as a test of fellowship, or membership in a Christian church. These fundamental distinctions were made clear in the early years of our reformatory movement, and its whole subsequent history has been shaped by their influence.

It is plain, then, that Mr. Campbell never thought of founding a community to reflect and perpetuate his own theological opinions. He fastened his opinions upon no one, in any way. In the department of opinion, of theology, he left every man as free as Christ had left him, and bravely insisted that none should be permitted to destroy or abridge that freedom. When he rested from his labors, there was not a single individual, or church, on earth, in any wise pledged to any theory or interpretation which he had held and promulgated by word or pen. The Disciples, his brethren, acknowledged and do acknowledge no leader, in the sense of the above-quoted motto, but the Lord Messiah. They have never been pledged to anything but the revealed truth of God, as each single soul finds it for himself, through whatever helping instrumentalities, in the Scriptures of the Old and New Testaments. Truth only has authority. Truth is eternal reality, as God sees it, in the kingdom of the Spirit. The soul of man is bound to this truth, and to naught besides. It is bound to the Holy Scriptures because they contain this truth. It is bound to Christ, who is the truth, and to his word, whether spoken by himself or others as the expression of that truth for the authoritative direction of human life. That which is the substance and essence of Christianity, the facts concerning Christ, the sincere and intelligent belief of these facts, the reverent trust in Christ superinduced through this belief, the new life of the soul divinely inbreathed by means of this belief and trust, the expression of this life in all piety Godward, and in all philanthropy manward — these are the things to which we are committed as a religious community, because these are the things bound upon us by the Head of the church, our Savior and Lord. To demand more than this, is to become a sect; to demand less, is to cease to be Christian. So all the Disciples of Christ understand the matter, and so have they ever understood it from Alexander Campbell down to him whose pen traces these words. In these things, our indebtedness to Mr. Campbell, under God, is very great, and is most cheerfully acknowledged. Further than these things we are not bound.

Mr. Campbell was a voluminous writer, but as editor of a religious periodical, rather than a maker of books. He became an editor early in his public career. His conception of the Christian religion was a growth. Like every other reformer, in cutting loose from the prescriptions of accepted creeds, he had to trace anew the great lines of Christian truth for himself. He says of his progress, that it "was gradual as the dawn." The great outlines, once distinctly grasped, had to be wrought out in detail patiently. What he thought and said at one time was not always strictly consistent with what he said at another. It is not a pleasant thing to confess one's mistakes, and though Mr. Campbell never, so far as the writer knows, said of any particular sentence he had written; "This was a mistake;" yet he revised his work so often, and surveyed the questions concerning which he wrote, from so many different points of view, that it is easy enough now to separate his mature and final utterances from those which were tentative, and intended to be accepted as provisional in their character. For instance, Mr. C. said some things in the *Christian Baptist* against Missionary, and even Bible Societies, which, at a later period, we positively know he would not have said. In his celebrated *Extras* on remission and regeneration, he expressed his views incautiously, and so as to do himself injustice, even if we grant that the position he intended to maintain was, for substance, the true one. So, also, in the dialogue of Timothy and Austin on the work of the Holy Spirit, he exposed himself not only to misrepresentation but even to honest misapprehension upon the part of many persons by whom he sincerely desired to be correctly understood. It seems only the part of candor to say these things now, when the battle is over, and the smoke of the conflict passing away. But one can have little patience with the wholesale misrepresentations which, in certain quarters, arose over these matters, and the obstinate unwillingness to be set right in regard to them, which was long persisted in by many fairly good men. If it cannot be set down to the account of inevitable human weakness, then no excuse can be made for it.

But the point is this: No man among the Disciples is in any wise bound to defend any position of Mr. Campbell's which he may honestly regard as untenable. Nor are our children trained in catechisms which imply their correctness, and so forestall the honest, independent judgment, to which their own investigations might lead them in their maturer years. We have no articles of faith shaped for us by Mr. Campbell, or any other uninspired man. And as a matter of fact, there is not one of us who does not exercise the freedom, which is our heritage, to the fullest extent which sincere and reverent personal investigation may seem to demand. Our relation to Mr. Campbell, and our other great men, is not at all that of the Lutheran Church to Luther, of the Calvinian churches to Calvin, or of the Methodist churches to John Wesley. This fact is now plain beyond honest — shall I say? — denial. Hence, it concerns us not in the least to know from whom Mr. Campbell may have learned this or that item in his theological system, or whether Sandeman and McLean were the real founders of the movement, which, in this country, has been generally connected with his name by those who oppose it. Our only concern is to know if it is, primarily, from God. If so we are satisfied. Short of this there is no resting-place to us; beyond this we have not the least wish to go.

And yet, as we understand it, our obligations to Mr. Campbell are such that his good name is a matter of some concern to us. We owe him, under God, as we feel, a great debt, and we should not be true to our manhood if we failed to repel the unfounded assertions of anyone who seeks to darken with dishonor his grand life. Someone once said, "How can you reply to a sneer?" Ah! Indeed! That has been my only difficulty in this review. Prof. Whitsitt's words of criticism and argument have been easily met. But there is more in his book — or I am much mistaken — than the words which convey his strictures upon Mr. Campbell and the Disciples. There is the out-breathing of a spirit, the effluence of a personality — not an "aureole," for that is from without, and suggests saintly sanctity, but an efflux, an emanation, which comes from within, and reveals the moods of the soul which sends it forth; and this is what has been hard to reply to in a way to realize my ideal of what a review should be. I have sincerely desired to be just. I should scorn to impute motives, in any case, less worthy than the real ones. But I have been unable in reading Prof. Whitsitt's little volume to escape this malodorous presence for many moments together. The bitter curl of the author's lip, the sardonic smile, the alternating scowl, "the slow-moving" index finger — these have kept themselves constantly before my mind's eye. If I have spoken any word "unadvisedly," if any expression stronger than truth required has at any time escaped me, then this sinister, impalpable "geist," which has constantly confronted me with its presence, is altogether to blame for it.

But I must repeat the fact that the Disciples are in no wise bound to any of Mr. Campbell's opinions, interpretations, or reasonings. Neither does our respect for him sensibly influence us in our search for truth in the Word of God. Our only quest is truth. Our practical aim is the glory of God. In the spirit of true disciples of the Master, we would seek the enlightenment and salvation of men. In all these things we are precisely as free as we should have been if Mr. Campbell had never lived. In a sense, Mr. Campbell was a great leader in our movement, but he has done what no other reformer ever did, he has left us our whole freedom in Christ, nay, he has eloquently and earnestly besought us to maintain this freedom, steadfast to the end. Our loyalty is due to Christ. And if, in the progress of knowledge, the pursuit of truth should lead us quite away from some of the chief land-marks of our early history, there is nothing under heaven to hold us back. We are pledged only to the faith in Christ which saves the soul, and that expression of this faith in the life, which makes salvation an assured possession, according to the word of our God. We cannot forsake this and be Christian; we cannot add to this, as a test of membership, without making ourselves another sect, among sects, and so forfeiting our birthright, as restorers of the original gospel.

With our Baptist brethren we have no unchristian quarrel. If they fail to see the ineffable dignity of our distinctive position, we are sorry enough that it is so, but we shall not, I trust, foolishly abuse them for it. They will see it in the Lord's own good time. It is as true now as it ever was, that only they can come to Christ, or to larger measures of the truth of Christ, who are drawn by the Father, and come because they are drawn. We earnestly desire to live in kindliest relations with the Baptists of all schools, and will so live, if they will only let us. But let them not delude themselves as to the reason that impels us to seek pleasant relations with them. We care as little for their endorsement as they can possibly care for ours. We know that we have the advantage of them before earth and heaven. We have moved on before them, in the grand march of human souls away from the superstitions and fantasies which yet survive the long spiritual night of the world, in which they had their birth. As men disengage themselves, more and more, from these unhappy survivals, the growth and power of our movement is bound to increase. If God so wills, we can afford to wait for the better day which is sure to come. And we can do without anybody's recognition, meantime, that gives it not at all, or only grudgingly. But our broad, divine plea compels us to hold our arms open for brotherhood and fellowship with those who sincerely love and serve our Lord, whether they see very clearly the genius of the common faith or not. It is not for us, who providentially occupy the vanguard of the Lord's moving hosts, to withhold our love from those who would fall into line with us, if they only saw clearly that they ought to do it. To speak boldly the truth which God has given us in charge, and to lovingly and patiently wait for its final triumph is our bounden duty. The blessing of the Lord God Almighty upon every soul that sincerely loves Jesus and seeks to follow in his footsteps.

APPENDIX

A Review by Henry C. Vedder[1]

The following extracts from an article by Dr. Henry C. Vedder, published in the number for July, 1888, of the *Baptist Quarterly Review*, will be a read with interest, as an expression of Baptist opinion:

Dr. Whitsitt begins by stating his thesis as follows:

> *"The Disciples of Christ, commonly called Campbellites from the name of their founder, Mr. Alexander Campbell, of Bethany, West Virginia, are an offshoot of the Sandemanian sect of Scotland."*

The value of this study of the sources from which the peculiar tenets and customs of the Disciples were drawn, so far as they were drawn immediately from other Christians and not immediately from the Scriptures, does not depend in the least upon the establishment of this proposition. This is fortunate, ***for it does not seem that the author has proved his thesis***."[2]

In the first place, the term 'offshoot' in Dr. Whitsitt's thesis does not seem to be very fortunately chosen. It seems to imply [does it not unqualifiedly and absolutely imply?] that there was an organic connection between the Sandemanian sect and the Disciples. ***This is by no means the case***.

> *"Thomas Campbell came to this country in 1807, a minister of the Seceders' Church, in full fellowship. Alexander Campbell, up to the time of his leaving Scotland, was also in full fellowship with this body, although in heart he had ceased to hold its doctrines, or to sympathize with its practice. He had spent some time, while a student at the University of Glasgow, in the society of Greville Ewing, one of the leaders of the Sandemanian sect, and had been strongly influenced by the peculiar notions of this able and eccentric divine. Many of these notions were afterwards worked out in the Reformation."*

His obligations to Ewing, and to the writings of Glas and Sande-

---

[1] Vedder is the author of several books, including *A History of the Baptists in the Middle States*.

[2] Bold font added for emphasis.

man, Alexander Campbell never denied or concealed. He did not profess that his teachings were original. He only claimed that they were true. "I am," said he, "greatly indebted to all the reformers, from Martin Luther down to John Wesley. I could not enumerate or particularize the individuals, living and dead, who have assisted in forming my mind. If all the Hebrew, Greek, Roman, Persian, French, English, Irish, Scotch, and American teachers and authors were to demand their own from me, I do not know that I would have two mites to buy incense to offer upon the altar to my genius of originality for the honors vouchsafed me."

****

This brief outline of facts is sufficient to show that, so far from being an "offshoot" of the Sandemanian sect of Scotland, the Disciples are, so far as any organic connection is concerned, an offshoot of the Baptist denomination of the United States. It might easily be shown, of course, that Alexander Campbell and his followers were nothing more than nominal Baptists. From the beginning they were never in sympathy with the views of truth that prevail among Baptist churches, but the fact is indisputable that they were in organic union with the Baptists until that union was dissolved by the Baptist associations and Baptist churches withdrawing fellowship from them.

The utmost, then, that Dr. Whitsitt's thesis can mean is, that in spirit, in doctrine and in church order the Disciples have drawn more largely from the Sandemanians than from any other body of Christians.

****

In Chapter II, of his little book he gives fifteen particulars of Sandemanian doctrines and practices, as follows:

1. ***A plurality of elders in each church.***
2. ***A weekly observance of the Lord's Supper.***
3. *The supporting of themselves by the elders in some trade or profession outside of the ministry.*
4. *The observance of love feasts such as prevailed in the early Christian Church.*
5. *The kiss of charity as enjoined in the apostolic letters.*
6. *Feet-washing as a church ordinance.*
7. *Abstinence from eating blood.*
8. *The necessity of absolute unanimity on the part of the various members in every transaction by an individual church.*
9. *A modified communism, the personal estate of each communicant being always subject to the demand of the necessitous, especially those of the household of faith.*

10. The calling of the weekly collection the fellowship,

11. *THE CUSTOM OF MUTUAL EXHORTATION AS A REGULAR PART OF RELIGIOUS WORSHIP.*

12. *Non-practice of family worship.*

13. *The absence of scruples against going to the theatre, or joining in the dance, or other social amusements with any, even with irreligious people.*

14. *THE EXCLUSION OF ALL BUT COMMUNICANTS FROM THE PUBLIC SERVICES OF THE CHURCH.*

15. The refusal to regard the first day of the week as a Sabbath, or to even call it by that name.

Dr. Whitsitt compares those peculiarities with the teachings of Mr. Campbell and the practice of the Disciples at the present time, with this curious result: Of the fifteen particulars enumerated, the Disciples agree with the Sandemanians in the four printed in bold, viz., numbers 1, 2, 10, and 15. The Disciples absolutely disagree with the Sandemanians in the nine particulars printed in ordinary type, viz., numbers 3, 4, 5, 6, 7, 8, 9, 12, and 13; and two cases printed in small capitals (11 and 14) are doubtful. *Ergo*, the Disciples are an "offshoot" of the Sandemanians!

****

But Dr. Whitsitt, in spite of his own confessions to the contrary, and in spite of facts that cannot be denied, persists in calling the Scotch Baptists, *Sandemanians* — "the immersed wing of the Sandemanian fraternity," and again, "the immersed Sandemanians," and similar titles. The more reasonable ground would seem to be that, after he severed his relations with the Sandemanian church at Glasgow, Archibald McLean was no more a Sandemanian than Adoniram Judson continued to be a Congregationalist, after he was baptized at Calcutta. It is necessary, however, for Dr. Whitsitt to maintain his views of McLean's continued connection with the Sandemanians, because otherwise his thesis utterly falls to the ground. The main ideas in Alexander Campbell's Reformation were, as he believes, borrowed from McLean, especially the distinctive and peculiar doctrine of baptism for the remission of sins; but McLean was, it seems plain, a Baptist when he wrote his *Commission of Christ*. Dr. Whitsitt's thesis as to the origin of the Disciples is in the predicament of Humpty Dumpty.

What Dr. Whitsitt calls the second stage of Mr. Campbell's perversion to Sandemanianism was the adoption of the views afterward advocated by him with regard to baptism. It seems that in the church at Brush Run, one of the most influential members, Joseph Bryant, was in favor of immersion. It became necessary, says Dr. Whitsitt, in order to secure his support and to prevent the church from going to pieces, that this question should be definitely decided:

> *He therefore resolved to take the step which it was becoming evident the larger portion of the church demanded at the hands of himself and his father. Accordingly he made preparations to procure his own immersion. When he went to communicate his intention to his father, an ally was found in the house in the person of his sister Dorothea. Naturally concerned to avoid an explosion in the church, by means of which she might be required to decide between the affection she bore her parents and her affection for the man to whom she was, perhaps, already betrothed, she had become, like Mr. Bryant, a decided advocate of immersion. If Mr. Bryant, and the majority of the little church at Brush Run, could have been induced to tolerate aspersion, it is probable that the Campbells would never have found it convenient to leave the side of the sprinkling Sandemanians.*

This is our author's account of a change, by all means the most important that ever occurred in the belief and practice of Alexander Campbell — a change that he always insisted was due to his conscientious convictions, growing out of an independent study of the Scriptures. Two of the least creditable motives that could possibly actuate a man in the matter of a religious conversion, are attributed in this account to Mr. Campbell: That he professed a change of convictions with reference to baptism, first, in order to retain the support of influential members of his church, and, second, to make sure of an eligible suitor for his sister's hand. To justify such accusations against the motives of any reputable Christian man, the strongest evidence ought to be produced. In favor of the first, Dr. Whitsitt produces only the fact that some members of the church strongly favored immersion. In favor of the second he has nothing better than a "perhaps." There is no evidence that Mr. Bryant was a suitor for Dorothea Campbell's hand before her baptism, and certainly none that, if he was a suitor, either of the Campbells was influenced by that fact.

But this is not all. Dr. Whitsitt gives us also an account, entirely original with him, of Alexander Campbell's change of views with regard to the subjects of baptism. It has already been disproved by the summary given from Mr. Richardson's narrative; but it is worthwhile to quote it, to show how completely the facts have been misinterpreted:

On the 13th of March, 1812, his first child was born. The question of infant baptism, therefore, became to him a topic of special interest. Doubtless with reference to the scruples of James Foster, he had formerly urged that this point should be treated as a matter of forbearance. That was the utmost limit to which he might safely advance if he desired to obtain the sympathy and support of so important a personage. It does not appear that he ventured as far as that since the 5th of June, 1811, possibly abstaining through fear of promoting an undesirable conflict. If now he had dared to baptize his child, after its birth in March, 1812, he must have done so with the conviction that the act would cost him the affections and countenance of most of the communicants at Brush Run. At any rate, he could not make up his mind to provoke the church in that way; and contrary to the position of Greville Ewing, his child was compelled to dispense with baptism.

The mention of James Foster's scruples is entirely gratuitous, for it was the fundamental position of the church at Brush Run from its organization, that the question of infant baptism was a "matter of indifference." There is not a circumstance in the whole of Alexander Campbell's life that gives the slightest warrant for the imputation against his courage. It would be difficult to name the other man in the history of modern Christianity who has shown a greater intrepidity, a more utter disregard of the opinions and prejudices of other men, a more unflinching determination to follow whithersoever his convictions pointed the way, than Alexander Campbell. Baptists believe that he was often in the wrong, but he was never a coward.

Dr. Jeter, one of his most active contemporary opponents, does him justice, when he says, "About this time (1811), he was led to question the divine authority of infant sprinkling, and, after a long, serious, and prayerful examination of all the sources of information within his reach, to reject it and to solicit immersion on a profession of faith." This is doubtless the exact truth, and the testimony is of the higher value, as it came from one who was, through most of his life, a vigorous opponent of Mr. Campbell's teachings.

It is with the utmost regret that these strictures are made upon Dr. Whitsitt's book. All of the present writer's prepossessions were in its favor, and it would have been a much more pleasant task to commend without qualification, than to dispute the statements of so eminent a scholar of our denomination. But the accomplished author would be the first to assert that truth is the highest of all considerations, and solely to help establish the truth these criticisms are made.

New York.
Henry C. Vedder.

The New York [Baptist] Examiner

The following paragraphs are taken from a Review in the *New York Examiner* (Baptist paper), of May 17, 1888. The writer shows clearly his Baptist sympathies, but evidently means to do justice. From a Baptist, this review is very significant:

> *Neither Alexander Campbell nor Thomas Campbell was ever a member of the Sandemanian sect. Both were, up to the time of their leaving Scotland, members of the Seceder Church, now known as the United Presbyterian Church. It is true that while at Glasgow University Alexander Campbell had been brought in contact with the Sandemanians, and had even imbibed some of their peculiar notions, which were worked out in his "Reformation," but a Sandemanian he never was. The Disciples are not an "offshoot" of the Sandemanians in any such sense as the Methodists may be called an offshoot of the Church of England. The connection between them, such as it is, is limited to spirit and doctrine. So far as outward and organic connection is concerned, the Disciples might much more plausibly be held to be an offshoot of the Baptist denomination.*

This reviewer then proceeds to state what he regards as the extent of Mr. Campbell's indebtedness to Sandeman. Concerning the points mentioned he adds the following:

> *These are the principal items that Mr. Campbell derived from the Sandemanians. None of them, excepting perhaps the first, is fundamental, as will readily be seen. The fundamental principles of the Disciple faith and practice, so far as they were borrowed, were derived from another source.*

Then he proceeds to administer a merited rebuke to Dr. W. for his illiberal and unjust treatment of the Scotch Baptists, as follows:

> *These he persists, in spite of proofs furnished in his own pages to the contrary, in calling "the immersed wing of the Sandemanian fraternity," "the immersed Sandemanians," and the like. Now it is quite true that at one time Robert Carmichael and Archibald McLean, the leaders of the Scotch Baptists, were connected with*

the Sandemanian persuasion. But both left the sect, Mr. Carmichael resigning the pastorate of the Sandemanian church in Glasgow, and Mr. McLean retiring from membership at the same time. "After this pair of friends had fallen into a condition of separation from the Sandemanians," to use Dr. Whitsitt's own words, he continues to call them Sandemanians; and this, too, after they had come to adopt believers' baptism, and had been themselves immersed on profession of their faith. That they no longer regarded themselves as Sandemanians, that the Sandemanians denounced them as Anabaptists, is no barrier to our author's fixed purpose that they shall be Sandemanians; and Sandemanians he calls them to the end. In our judgment this is not historical criticism, it is not fair treatment of the facts.

The following extract is especially noteworthy, but only what simple honesty required at the reviewer's hands:

The account given in chapter VIII. of Mr. Campbell's adoption of immersion as baptism and rejection of infant baptism is greatly to be regretted. There is no good reason — certainly Dr. Whitsitt produces none — to doubt the statement of Mr. Campbell's biographer that this step was taken after protracted study of the Scriptures, and much heart-searching on the part of both the Campbells. Professor Richardson gives a long and circumstantial narrative of the causes that led to this action, and unless that narrative is an entire fabrication, the imputations of unworthy motives made by Dr. Whitsitt have no foundation of fact, and should be expunged from his book.

It was natural that a Baptist reviewer should find in a book like Dr. Whitsitt's some things to be commended. These are duly noted, and at least as much credit given as is deserved. It is enough that this distinguished Baptist says that Prof. Whitsitt has not proved his main thesis — that which his book was meant to prove; and that an important section of it brought injustice to the truth of history, and ought to be expunged. The Disciples need ask no more.